A Curious Student's Guide to the Book of Numbers

A Curious Student's Guide to the Book of Numbers

Enduring Life Lessons for the Twenty-First Century

REUVEN TRAVIS

WIPF & STOCK · Eugene, Oregon

A CURIOUS STUDENT'S GUIDE TO THE BOOK OF NUMBERS
Enduring Life Lessons for the Twenty-First Century

Copyright © 2021 Reuven Travis. All rights reserved. Except for brief quotations in critical publications or reviews, no part of this book may be reproduced in any manner without prior written permission from the publisher. Write: Permissions, Wipf and Stock Publishers, 199 W. 8th Ave., Suite 3, Eugene, OR 97401.

Wipf & Stock
An Imprint of Wipf and Stock Publishers
199 W. 8th Ave., Suite 3
Eugene, OR 97401

www.wipfandstock.com

PAPERBACK ISBN: 978-1-6667-0673-4
HARDCOVER ISBN: 978-1-6667-0674-1
EBOOK ISBN: 978-1-6667-0675-8

10/15/21

Original illustrations by Eli Portman.

In Appreciation to
Rabbi Michael J. Broyde

It is a miracle that curiosity survives formal education.

—Albert Einstein

Contents

Acknowledgements | ix
Preface for Parents and Educators | xi
Introduction for the Curious Student | xxi

Bamidbar
    Part One (For Parents and Educators): Role Models | 1
    Part Two: Organizing the Camp | 7
Naso | 15
Beha'alotecha | 25
Shelach | 39
Korach | 51
Chukat | 63
Balak | 77
    Part One (For Parents and Educators): Who is the Greater Prophet, Moses or Balaam? | 77
    Part Two: Turning Curses into Blessings | 80
Pinchas | 91
Matot | 103
Massei | 113

About the Author | 119
Bibliography | 121

Acknowledgements

I truly do not have the words to express the gratitude I owe Rabbi Michael J. Broyde. For many years, he has been my teacher and mentor. Throughout my career as an educator, I could always turn to him for advice and could always count on his support, even at times when support for me professionally was in short supply. Last but certainly not least, he is a good friend. The frequent phone calls I get from him just to ask, "Hi, how are you?" or "Is there anything I should be doing for you?" mean more to me than he could imagine.

This book is dedicated to him with deep respect and admiration.

One other "thank you" is in order. As was the case with the two previous books in this series, my friend and colleague Lisa Marks has been a great help. She is a gifted educator, and her insights and suggestions about this book were always right on the mark. (Bad pun, I know, but Lisa is a big fan of bad puns.)

Rabbi Reuven Travis

Preface for Parents and Educators

Readers of my previous books on Genesis and Exodus might have assumed that my next project would involve the book of Leviticus, the third of the five books that make up the Torah. Yet when it comes to teaching the Torah to elementary school-age students, whether in a day school or in a Sunday school setting, it is common to skip the book of Leviticus and move directly to the book of Numbers after completing Genesis and Exodus. A quick perusal of Leviticus makes clear why this is so.

Much of Leviticus focuses on the sacrificial rites performed in the tabernacle (or *mishkan*, as it is called in Hebrew), which can seem quite foreign to the modern reader and incomprehensible to children. Leviticus also sets forth, as a corollary to the sacrificial laws, those commandments pertaining to ritual purity and impurity, a topic of extreme complexity and limited relevance in modern times.[1] Leviticus contains a detailed discussion of prohibited sexual relationships, a topic not at all appropriate for young children. It has a similarly detailed description of the Jewish dietary laws, which have little meaning to non-Jews and, frankly, to many Jews.[2] Even the narrative portions of Leviticus, such as the

---

1. Like the laws governing the sacrificial rites, those governing ritual purity and impurity apply only when there is a temple in active use in Jerusalem.

2. According to data compiled by the American Jewish Committee in 2018, 11 percent of American Jewish households are Orthodox and presumably observe Jewish dietary laws. According to a 2013 Pew Research Center Study on

Preface for Parents and Educators

story of the deaths of Aaron's two oldest sons, are difficult even for adults to grasp and process.[3]

In comparison to Leviticus, the book of Numbers may seem like an easy text to teach children. But it also presents challenges, for both practical and theological reasons.[4]

Let's start with the nature of God. Christians and Jews alike teach their children that the God they worship is merciful. Yet, as previously mentioned, it is easy to read Numbers as a story of a sinful people and a wrathful God. The God of Numbers certainly seems to see it this way:

> Nevertheless, as I live and as the LORD's Presence fills the whole world, none of the men who have seen My Presence and the signs that I have performed in Egypt and in the wilderness, and who have tried Me these many times and have disobeyed Me, shall see the land

---

American Jewish beliefs and practices, 31 percent of Jews who identified as Conservative reported that they kept kosher. This same study reported that 7 percent of Reform respondents upheld the practice, while 10 percent of those who claimed no particular affiliation kept kosher in the home. Added together, these figures suggest that only one in five American Jews observe some form of the Torah's dietary restrictions.

3. The beginning of the tenth chapter of Leviticus describes their deaths as follows: "Now Aaron's sons Nadab and Abihu each took his fire pan, put fire in it, and laid incense on it; and they offered before the LORD alien fire, which He had not enjoined upon them. And fire came forth from the LORD and consumed them; thus they died at the instance of the LORD." Despite the seemingly simple reading of the text—that is, they died because they offered a sacrifice without being commanded to do so (hence, an "alien fire")—the midrash and the traditional commentators offer many other rationales for their deaths, such as: they entered the tabernacle while intoxicated; they were not wearing all the priestly garments when they offered up this incense; they refrained from having children; they refrained even from marrying; they adjudicated legal matters in the presence of their teacher Moses; and they openly discussed that they would assume leadership positions upon the deaths of Moses and Aaron. To describe this as a much-discussed and little-understood story would not be an overstatement.

4. The discussion that follows is culled from my previous work *Sefer Bamidbar as Sefer HaMiddot: The Book of Numbers as the Book of Character Development* (WIPF & Stock, 2018).

Preface for Parents and Educators

that I promised on oath to their fathers; none of those who spurn Me shall see it. (Num 14:21–23)

How many is "many?" It is easy enough to count. Starting with chapter 14 of the book of Exodus and continuing through chapter 14 of the book of Numbers, the Torah mentions ten incidents that seem to underscore the rebellious nature of the Jewish people in the Sinai desert.[5] It would thus seem that God's wrath is justified. But where is the merciful God we teach our children about?

For many Christian preachers and teachers, there is no theological dilemma here. They view the God of the Old Testament as a God of wrath, whereas the God of the New Testament is seen as a God of love. Carl Olson, editor of *Catholic World Report* and *Ignatius Insight*, sums it up quite succinctly when he states that there is a "widespread and deeply ingrained" view among some Christians "that the God described in the Old Testament is, on the whole, quite angry and judgmental."[6]

Chuck Swindoll expresses a similar view. Swindoll is an evangelical Christian pastor, author, educator, and radio preacher who founded the publication *Insight for Living* and a radio program of the same name that airs on more than two thousand stations around the world. In his words, "More than just a history lesson, the Book of Numbers reveals how God reminded Israel that He does not tolerate rebellion, complaining, and disbelief without invoking consequences."[7]

To their credit, authors such as Olson and Swindoll work to disabuse the masses of this image of a wrathful and unforgiving God. Their efforts make sense if one sees in the Old Testament theological underpinnings to the New Testament, and even a cursory perusal of the internet will show the extent to which Christian leaders strive to instill in their followers the notion that there is one God, whose anger is tempered by mercy. As Swindoll writes, "Though the people failed many times, God showed His own

---

5. The Babylonian Talmud (Erchin 15a) has a detailed discussion of each of these incidents.
6. Olson, "Angry God."
7. Swindoll, "Numbers."

Preface for Parents and Educators

faithfulness by His constant presence leading the way: through a cloud by day and a pillar of fire by night."[8] For Swindoll, God's mercy extends beyond taking care of the physical needs of the Jewish people. He is equally concerned with their spiritual needs. "He taught His people how to walk with Him—not just with their feet through the wilderness, but with their mouths in worship, hands in service, and lives as witnesses to the surrounding nations."[9]

Like their Christian counterparts, Jewish sages and scholars also address the difficulties inherent to the notion of a seemingly wrathful God. The Bible has many examples of God's wrathful anger, and the talmudic sages went so far as to proclaim that "as long as the wicked exist in the world, there is wrath in the world."[10] Nonetheless, the insights by Jewish scholars throughout the centuries into the Bible and its stories of a wrathful God have been driven and colored by the longstanding tradition of a God whose mercy is essentially limitless and who far more often than not allows His mercy to trump both His anger and His desire to dole out strict justice.

Try parsing this for children!

When it comes to teaching Numbers to children, this tension between a wrathful and merciful God is perhaps more evident than in any book of the Bible, and it begs a straightforward but not so simple question: How does one reconcile the rebellious behavior of the Jewish people in the wilderness (and the subsequent anger of and punishment by God) found in Numbers with the foundational principle of a merciful God?

Rabbi Ovadyah Sforno tackles this question in his introduction to the book of Numbers. He explains that this book is largely about the interplay between strict justice (exhibited by God's wrath and punishments) and mercy (seen in God's forgiveness of rebellious behavior), and he points to several well-known narratives in Numbers to prove his point.[11] Take, for example, the episode involving the "mixed multitude" of nations (Num 11:4–6). These

8. Swindoll, "Numbers."
9. Swindoll, "Numbers."
10. B. Sanh. 111b.
11. Sforno, *Commentary*, 640–41.

Preface for Parents and Educators

individuals, who accompanied the Jewish people into the desert, complained about the lack of meat and, in doing so, prompted the Jews themselves to complain as well. Sforno argues that the people did not actually complain in their hearts, because they had nothing to complain about. They only voiced complaints as a way of testing God. As such, are they not deserving of God's wrath?

In his commentary on this episode, Rabbi Shlomo ben Yitzhak (better known as Rashi) takes a similar approach. He maintains that the people were deliberatively provocative and that their complaints were not really about meat. Rather, the people were seeking a pretext to turn away from God—and not just any pretext, but one that would seem evil in to Him and thus provoke Him. Relying on midrashic sources, Rashi suggests that the people said something akin to "Woe is to us! How weary we have become on this journey! For three days, we have not rested from the fatigue of walking."

And how does God react to this deliberate provocation? "The people took to complaining bitterly before the LORD. The LORD heard and was incensed: a fire of the LORD broke out against them, ravaging the outskirts of the camp."

Yes, God becomes angry. And, yes, the fire of God burns in them, and it consumes the edge of the camp. Then the story continues, "the people cried out to Moses. Moses prayed to the LORD, and the fire died down" (Num 11:2). Thus, in the end, Sforno's premise about the book of Numbers proves true. The people's complaints are misguided, and their provocation of God is deliberate. Justice demands that the people be punished and punished harshly. Yet, the call for justice is tempered by God's mercy. When God hears the cries of the people and the prayers of Moses, He causes the fire to die down.

Why does God give the Jewish people another chance? Why does He allow His merciful attributes to overshadow His desire for strict justice? The answer is simple. God gives the people another chance so that they may prepare themselves properly for their next opportunity for redemption.

This tempering of justice with mercy is be demonstrated again and again in the Bible. It is consistent with both the Jewish

Preface for Parents and Educators

belief in a merciful God and the Christian belief that the God of the Old Testament is the same loving and merciful God of the New Testament. It also forms the basis for a reasoned and compelling understanding of the narrative of Numbers. Adults can and often do arrive at such a reading. In contrast, it can be very challenging to help children see Numbers in the same light. Yet, it is a challenge that must be taken up if we are to teach children to be curious and inquisitive when reading the Torah. That fact that a given story (or perhaps even an entire book) might provoke difficult or sometimes even unanswerable questions is no reason not to teach a text as rich and meaningful as Numbers.

By now, it should be clear that an obvious but arguably simplistic approach to looking at Numbers is to see it as a story of a sinful people and a wrathful God. There may be a measure of truth to this, and, indeed, a simple approach may often be best when teaching children. However, my many years in education have shown me that teaching Numbers in an overly simplistic manner is ill-advised, even when working with younger students. This book was written with this thought in mind: that parents and educators can teach Numbers seriously even to young students and that by doing so, they can impart to children many important life lessons that Numbers has to offer.

Maximizing the utility of this book as you share it with your children and students necessitates a few more observations.

A significant challenge in teaching children the books of the Torah is this differentiating between the text itself and the accompanying biblical exegesis. This is particularly tricky in Jewish homes and schools where adults often turn to midrash (a form of biblical exegesis developed and employed by ancient Judaic authorities) as a tool for helping children better understand the biblical narrative. Midrash provides us with important insights into and backstories to the text, but students should never conflate it with the Bible itself. The biblical text is the text, and midrash is commentary on the text.

When using midrash to make the text more easily understood (whether in the classroom or at home interacting with my

Preface for Parents and Educators

own children), I have always been guided by the approach of Rabbi Moshe ben Nachman, the great biblical commentator from the 1200s. In his famous disputation with the apostate Jew Pablo Christiani, Rabbi Moshe made this observation:

> We possess three genres of literature. The first is the Bible or Tanakh, and all of us believe in its words with a complete trust. The second is the Talmud, and it is an exposition of the commandments of the Torah, for the Torah contains 613 commandments. Not a single one of them is left unexplained by the Talmud. We believe in the Talmud with respect to its exposition of the commandments. The third type of book that we possess is the Midrash, and it is like sermons . . . Concerning this collection, for one who believes it, good. For one who does not believe it, there is no harm . . ."[12]

I have never been one to insist that students see midrashic expositions as accurate historical accounts, nor have I framed midrashic stories as mere parables. How a student chooses to see this literature is up to him or her. But what cannot be ignored or diminished are the important lessons the midrash offers us. Here are two well-known examples of the midrash's treatment of the Numbers narrative that illuminate this point.

Let's start with the manna, the heavenly bread that sustained the Jewish people throughout their forty-year sojourn in the wilderness. The text tells us that the manna was the size of a coriander seed and the color of a white *bedolach*, which is understood to be a fine crystal. The text goes on to describe the taste of the manna as akin to something fried in oil and honey. The midrash, however, has much more to say about the taste of the manna. According to the midrash, its taste somehow matched the taste needs and preferences of each individual. To adults, it tasted like adult food. For babies and infants, it had the taste of breastmilk. What's more, when one had a yen for a different food, be it beef, fruit, or grain, one needed only to "wish," and the manna's taste satisfied one's individual desire.

---

12. Ramban (Nahmanides), *The Disputation at Barcelona*, paragraph 39.

Preface for Parents and Educators

In the midrashic literature, the water source for the Jewish people as they travelled through the wilderness is equally miraculous.

Toward the end of their wanderings in the wilderness, the Jewish people arrive at the desert of Zin. It is there that Miriam dies and is buried. It is also there, we are told, that the people have no water and so assemble against Moses and Aaron.

The death of Miriam and the lack of water is an odd juxtaposition. This prompts the talmudic sages to conclude that there was a readily available water source, something they named "Miriam's well."[13] The midrash abounds with stories about this miraculous water source.

First, it is counted among the ten unique things the talmudic sages maintain were created at twilight on the eve of the first Shabbat after creation.[14]

Second, the midrash states that this "well" was actually a rock shaped like a sieve that would roll with the Jewish people as they marched through the wilderness. When they stopped, the rock would also stop and would burrow itself deep into the sand. The leaders of the tribes would come and stand by it, saying: "Rise up, O well," and it would rise.[15]

This rock described by the midrash is, of course, the very rock from which Moses first brought forth water when the Jewish people complained about their lack of water (Exod 17:3). It is also the same rock that, after Miriam dies, Moses hits in order to draw forth water once again (Num 20:2).

It is safe to say that virtually every Jewish child who has studied Numbers is familiar with the midrash's treatment of the manna and of Miriam's well. Learning these stories is both worthwhile and enlightening, but it is critical that students recognize them as midrash and understand that they are not found in the text of Numbers itself. (Throughout this book, when midrash is used to explain the text, it will be identified as such, or it will be referred to as "the rabbinic tradition.")

13. Taanit 9a.
14. Pirkei Avot 5:6.
15. Bamidbar Rabbah 1:1.

Preface for Parents and Educators

In addition to understanding how and when midrash is used in this book, readers should also be familiar with the approach I employ for presenting and examining the central stories of Numbers. In brief, I have opted not to use the system of chapters and verse numbers most students of the Bible are acquainted with. This division was first made in the Latin Bible in the thirteenth century, most likely by Stephen Langston.[16] Langston's system was employed in the concordances of the Vulgate, and this in turn gave Rabbi Isaac Nathan[17] the idea for the first Hebrew concordance. The citations in this concordance first give the number of the Vulgate chapter and then give the number of the masoretic[18] verse chapter, which remains to this day the standard format of the printed Hebrew Bible.

However, the printed format of the Hebrew Bible is not the one used for ritual purposes. As part of Jewish prayer services on the Sabbath, different portions of the Torah are read each week.[19] These readings are commonly referred to as the weekly *parasha* or *sedra*. The starting and ending points of each parasha have nothing at all to do with Langston's system for organizing the Bible. Rather, they reflect the long-standing masoretic tradition.

Given my background and training as an Orthodox Jewish rabbi and educator, it made sense for me to organize this book according to these weekly parashas. It is a system I know well and

---

16. Stephen Langton was an English cardinal of the Roman Catholic Church and Archbishop of Canterbury from 1207 to his death, in 1228. The dispute between King John of England and Pope Innocent III over his election as archbishop was a major factor in the crisis that produced the Magna Carta in 1215.

17. Rabbi Isaac Nathan ben Kalonymus was a French Jewish philosopher who lived in the fourteenth and fifteenth centuries. In the introduction to his concordance, Rabbi Isaac wrote that he was completely ignorant of the Bible until his fifteenth year. Prior to that time, his studies had been restricted to the Talmud and religious philosophy.

18. In rabbinic Judaism, the Masoretic Text is the authoritative Hebrew and Aramaic text of the Bible. It was copied, edited, and distributed primarily by a group of Jews known as the Masoretes between the seventh and tenth centuries CE.

19. There are fifty-four such weekly portions, which means that a double portion is read on some weeks.

Preface for Parents and Educators

am comfortable with. More important, these weekly readings, in my opinion, present a more logical flow for the major themes and stories of Numbers than do the chapter and verse numbers in common usage.[20]

Each chapter of this book opens with a brief overview and synopsis of the weekly Torah reading. Then will come a section I call "Life Lessons from This Week's Reading," which has the goal of helping young students think more deeply about the text read each week, as opposed to merely memorizing certain incidents from the narrative. Finally, there will be questions for students to think about as they begin to make the lessons from each week's reading their own.

To help parents and educators contextualize what I think of as "big picture" questions about Numbers, I have also included three chapters for adult readers of this book. (They are always referred to as "Part One" in discussions of the weekly readings.) One such chapter addresses the difference in character development between the protagonists as portrayed in Numbers and those in Genesis. A second deals with the talmudic debate regarding the comparative greatness of Moses and Balaam. The last wrestles with the issue of zealotry as it appears in the Phineas narrative.

All translations of biblical verses in this book are from *Tanakh: A New Translation of the Holy Scriptures according to the Traditional Hebrew Text*[21] unless otherwise indicated. This translation is available in the public domain and with a free public license thanks to Sefaria (www.sefaria.org), a nonprofit organization that, in its own words, is dedicated to assembling "a free, living library of Jewish texts."

---

20. Indeed, there are many chapter breaks that interrupt the logical flow of the narrative that the masoretic tradition avoids. See, for example, the end of chapter 43 and the beginning of chapter 44. This is clearly a single narrative—one we will discuss in great detail later in this book—and most modern editors would be confounded by the insertion of a new chapter here.

21. Philadelphia: Jewish Publication Society, 1985.

Introduction for the Curious Student

How many stories do you remember from the book of Genesis? Not sure? Here are a few you've probably heard of: Adam and Eve, Noah and the great flood, the tower of Babel, Abraham offering his son Isaac as a sacrifice, and Jacob tricking his father so he can take his brother Esau's blessing. Are there others you can think of?

What about the book of Exodus? You may be familiar with the stories of the Jews going down to Egypt and being enslaved there, the birth of Moses, Pharaoh's daughter saving baby Moses from the Nile River, Moses telling Pharaoh to let the Jews people go, the ten plagues, the splitting of the "Red Sea" (actually the Sea of Reeds), and God's giving the Ten Commandments at Mount Sinai.

Now think about the book of Numbers. It's probably a bit harder to remember its stories, because Numbers can be a hard book for children to learn. The Jewish people seem to challenge and disobey God time and time again in Numbers. God in turn gets angry with the Jewish people—so angry that He sometimes strikes down hundreds or even thousands of them with plagues.

The truth is, Numbers is a hard book, even for parents and teachers. Its stories are not always so clear-cut. They don't always have happy endings. They often leave us asking more questions than we have answers for.

This is why you may not have spent a lot of time studying or talking about Numbers. But it is also exactly why you should study Numbers.

Introduction for the Curious Student

The stories in Numbers, like life itself, aren't "black and white," with easy and obvious answers. Instead, its stories are "gray," meaning that there is often more than one way to understand and explain them.

Some find this "gray" to be confusing. But this book uses the multiple ways of looking at the stories in Numbers as tool for teaching you, the reader, how and when to ask questions. More important, it will try to show you that asking good questions is worthwhile even when there are no good answers to your questions.

Ready to tackle some interesting but challenging stories? Let's get started.

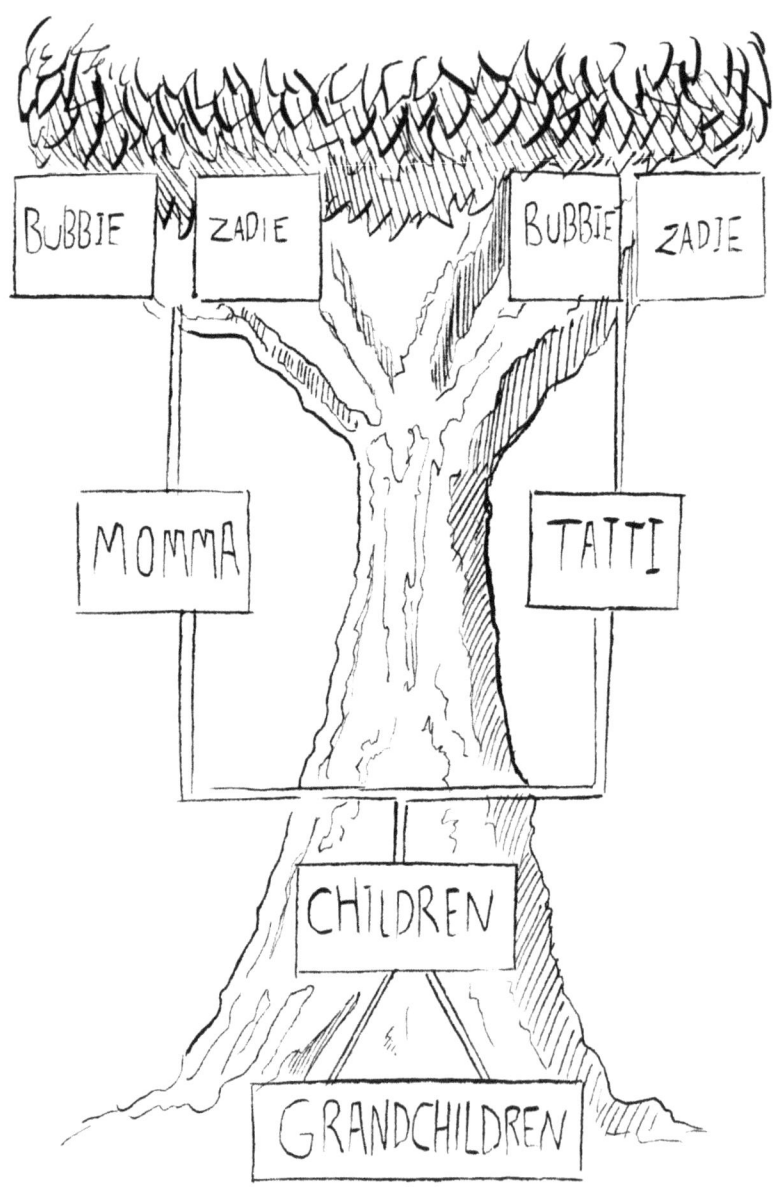

Bamidbar

(Num 1:1—4:20)

Part One (For Parents and Educators): Role Models

Anyone who has studied the Torah, whether as an adult or as a child, quickly understands that it has much more to offer than its many laws and commandments. Genesis, for example, has almost no laws[1] and contains instead two major storylines: how humankind came to be and the origins of the Jewish people. Exodus contains many commandments, in particular about the holiday of Passover and the construction of the Tabernacle. However, the first half of the book is all about the story of the enslavement of the Jews in Egypt and their ultimate exodus from there.[2]

The book of Numbers both follows and breaks this pattern. It, too, combines stories with laws, and while it is possible to view Numbers as one story, that is, the wanderings of the Jewish people in the wilderness for forty years, this approach misses the mark. The forty-year saga of the Jews' journey to the Holy Land is

---

1. Jewish tradition maintains that Genesis sets forth only three commandments: to have children ("be fruitful and multiply"), to circumcise male children on the eighth day (as commanded to Abraham), and not to eat the meat of the sciatic nerve (as a remembrance of Jacob wrestling with an angel).

2. The book of Leviticus breaks this pattern. It is, for the most part, devoted to the sacrificial rites performed in the *Mishkan* (Tabernacle). It does contain an important story about the deaths of Aaron's two oldest sons, Nadab and Abihu. However, unlike the two books of the Torah that precede it, Leviticus has no storylines that run throughout the book.

dominated by a series of stories that focus on individuals or small groups of people, such as Caleb, Korah, Balaam, Phinehas, and even the princes and the spies.

We will discuss and examine all their stories, but before we do, there is an important question to consider. Readers of the Torah see that the stories it contains are not mere historical retellings of events long past. The stories are meant to teach us life lessons and to show us how to be better people and live more meaningful lives. And when it comes to life lessons, many see Genesis as offering the best and most enduring examples.

Let's start at the beginning (please forgive the bad pun).

Many biblical commentators ask why the Torah, which is often thought of as a book of laws, begins with the creation story. Some see the creation story as necessary to teach that all of creation comes from God. Others see the story as establishing an important link between the Jewish people and the land of Israel.

Yet the many explanations as to why the creation story appears at the start of Genesis often do not touch on the rest of the book's stories. This leaves us to wonder why, for example, we need the stories of Cain and Abel, Noah and the flood, the tower of Babel, and the patriarchs and matriarchs. A widely accepted answer is that these stories are in the Torah to teach us about proper character traits.

Let's pause for a moment and define "character trait." A character trait is a part of a person's personality that helps make them into the kind of person they are. Kindness and friendliness are examples of good character traits.

Back to the stories. Once we accept that the idea of developing proper character traits is an important one, we can understand the need for the story of Cain and Abel. Its purpose is to show us how badly one might sin if overcome by jealousy. The story of Noah and the flood reminds us of what can happen when people will do whatever they want to get anything and everything they want. The story of the tower of Babel and the scattering of its builders teaches that chasing after excessive honor and glory can have terrible consequences.

Bamidbar (Num 1:1—4:20)

And what of the stories of the patriarchs (Abraham, Isaac, and Jacob) and the matriarchs (Sarah, Rebekah, Rachel, and Leah)? Their stories teach us the basics of serving God. In particular, these stories show us how one should develop and improve one's character traits so as fulfill the commandment set forth in Deut 6:18: "to do that which is upright and good in the eyes of the LORD," a commandment that is telling us to always try to do the right thing, no matter what the circumstances. It is thus not surprising that the Babylonian Talmud[3] refers to the book of Genesis as *Sefer hayyashar*, the "Book of the Upright," and to the patriarchs and matriarchs as the "Upright Ones."

Viewing Genesis as the "Book of the Upright" makes sense because its main characters are often seen as being very good or very bad. Take, for instance, Esau, Jacob's oldest son. There is little in the Torah that clearly depicts Esau as evil, yet the midrash is full of stories that emphasize his evil nature. In one midrash, he returns from the field famished.[4] A simple reading of the text would lead one to assume that Esau was hunting and that after being in the fields for a long time, he is simply hungry. Instead, the midrash maintains that his hunger and fatigue are due to the fact that he just committed his first terrible crime, the murder of Nimrod. Another midrash blames the blindness Isaac experiences late in life on the smoke from the sacrifices Esau's wives offer to their idols.

And the list goes on: Cain, Ishmael, Abimelech, Laban. These characters have nothing to offer us as role models, because they are seen in the rabbinic literature as completely wicked. Contrasting this are the patriarchs and their wives, whose lives and actions are often thought of as approaching perfection. Only they model proper behavior, and the model they present us is one of goodness and righteousness. It is as if there were only black and white in Genesis, no gray. The wicked are very wicked, and the good are very good. This is not a very sophisticated way to think of such things, but keeping it simple, portraying things as either black or

---

3. Avodah Zarah 25a.

4. The midrash here is examining the story found Gen 25 in which Esau sells his birthright to Jacob.

white, works well when teaching young children. It is thus not surprising that many see Genesis as the most important of the books of the Torah for teaching proper character traits to children (and even to adults as well).

But this is a book about Numbers. Where and how does Numbers fit into this idea of teaching proper character traits? After all, the book of Numbers is often thought of as little more than an extended history lesson. What does it have to do with teaching proper behavior?

Over the many years that I have worked as an educator, I have thought about this a lot, and I have come to the conclusion that in many ways, Numbers is even a better text than Genesis for teaching proper behavior. Here's why.

As children grow, they inevitably come to think about the type of people they want to be. Their parents, their teachers, and even their friends offer suggestions about (or criticisms of) their behaviors. "This is a good thing," children are told. "Keep doing it." Or "This is a bad thing. How could you do it?"

Compounding (and perhaps confusing) matters, children see different standards of acceptable behavior in the different spheres they inhabit. What is allowed at home may not be allowed at school. What they see at the mall or the grocery store or online is certainly not what they see in their houses of worship or their religiously oriented camps and youth groups.

If taught properly, the book of Numbers can help children make sense of such conflicting messages. This is because many of the behaviors and character traits children will ultimately wrestle with are treated in great detail in Numbers. However—and this is a key point—this treatment is often done in an indirect manner, that is, through a variety of character traits (sometimes good and sometimes bad) that themselves are presented via the diverse personality types that dominate the narrative of Numbers.

Want proof? Consider this. The name of each weekly Torah portion typically reflects the first distinctive word in the Hebrew text of the portion in question. And, as we will see, many of the weekly portions in Numbers are named for people. I do not believe this is coincidental. Rather, I believe that these weekly readings are named for these individuals precisely so that we focus on their personalities and their behaviors. In short, I believe (and hope to demonstrate in subsequent chapters) that the various personages in the book of Numbers are meant to be powerful examples of various character traits. The great challenge for students as they read and ponder the book is to determine whether these character traits are ones the Torah is encouraging us to adopt or to avoid.

A few examples will demonstrate this.

Without doubt, Korah's rebellion against the leadership of Moses is driven by jealousy.[5] Korah truly believes that he, not Aaron, deserves to be high priest. What's more, Korah is convinced that Aaron has the job simply because he is Moses's brother. These factors do not justify Korah's rebellion, but his issues seem very real to him. Not getting something you think you deserve and seeing someone else get it is exactly the kind of problem children can relate to and understand.

In comparison, Cain's jealousy and reactions are over the top and hard to relate to.[6] He kills his brother because his brother's offering is considered better! And he does so even after God encourages him to change course in Gen 4:6–7: "And the LORD said to Cain, '"Why are you distressed, And why is your face fallen? Surely, if you do right, There is uplift."' In essence, God says to Cain, try harder next time, and it will go better for you.

Then we have Phinehas. There can be no doubt that Phinehas is a religious hero. He alone steps up when the nation is facing

---

5. In chapters 17 and 18 of Numbers, we read how Korah incites a mutiny against Moses' leadership generally and against the appointment of Aaron as High Priest specifically. Korah is joined by 250 distinguished members of the community, who offer incense in the Tabernacle to prove their worthiness for the priesthood. The earth opens up in a miraculous manner and swallows the mutineers, and a fire consumes those who had offered the incense.

6. Adam and Eve were then expelled from the idyllic Garden of Eden. Eve gave birth to two sons, Cain and Abel. When Abel's offering to God was accepted, while Cain's was rejected, Cain murdered his brother in a jealous rage. God punished Cain, designating him to be a lifelong wanderer, but postponing his ultimate punishment for seven generations.

religious and moral crisis, not to mention God's wrath.[7] He acts while everyone else, at best, watches, and he risks his life by so doing. Nonetheless, the Jewish tradition does not easily or quickly embrace the actions of Phinehas. In an act of zealotry, he took it upon himself to be judge, jury, and executioner. His action may have assuaged God's angry, but the rabbis recognize that zealotry, the character trait Phinehas seems to embody, is dangerous. When passion and rage controls one's actions (as is typically the case with a zealot), things can easily spin out of control.

Unlike those in Genesis, the character traits embodied by key figures in Numbers are not black and white but very gray. Is jealousy always a bad thing, or can being jealous of my friend's successes motivate me to do better? Greed is certainly a bad trait, but doesn't a desire to earn more money prompt people to work harder? Being too boastful about one's accomplishments is discouraged, but don't people have a right to be proud of what they have achieved?

The gray that colors the life lessons we see in the book of Numbers can make them somewhat complicated, but it also makes them that much more memorable. But don't take my word for this. Read on and see for yourself!

---

7. Following Balaam's unsuccessful attempt to curse the Jewish nation (Num 22—24), he convinces the kings of Moab and Midian to send their daughters to seduce many Jewish men, and, in the course of doing so, entice them to worship the *Baal Peor* deity. God is understandably angry and commands Moses to execute the guilty people. God simultaneously sends a lethal plague to strike the Jews. As the plague sweeps through the camp, a Jewish leader, Zimri, shows his disdain for Moses and the other leaders by being physically intimate with a Midianite princess before their very eyes. All the leaders, including Moses, are shocked and are unable to react, except for Aaron's grandson, Phineas, who kills both Zimri and the Midianite princess. Phineas' action brings a halt to the plague.

Bamidbar

(Num 1:1—4:20)

Part Two: Organizing the Camp

Summary of This Week's Reading

This week's reading helps us understand why the book is called "Numbers": There's a lot of counting. God commands Moses to count the men of all the tribes (except Levi) who are old enough to serve in the army (which means ages twenty to sixty). The grand total is 603,550 men.

Moses is also commanded to count all males one month and older of the tribe of Levi. As part of this counting, Moses is to do two things: make sure he knows how many men there are in the three families that make up the tribe of Levi and not include any firstborn in this count. The total, excluding the firstborns, is 22,000.

After he counts the families of Levi, Moses assigns each family special jobs involving the tabernacle (or mishkan in Hebrew). The family of Gershon is in charge of transporting the tapestries and curtains and their accessories. The Kehot family is in charge of transporting all the holy vessels. The Merari family is in charge of carrying the beams, panels, and sockets.

There is one more count to go. God tells Moses to count all firstborn males from the twelve tribes. Why? Before the sin of the golden calf, firstborn males had a special status, and they would have had the honor of working in the mishkan. However, because of this terrible sin, that honor will now go to the tribe of Levi. When Moses finishes this count, he finds that there are 273 more firstborn males than the total number of males in Levi. God instructs Moses that each of these "extra" firstborns (as determined by a lottery) must give five shekels to the priests. In this way, these "extra" firstborns are "redeemed."

After all the counting is finished, Moses instructs the people on how they should organize themselves whenever it is time to set up camp. The tabernacle will be at the center of the camp, and there will be four "mini camps" around it. To the east, represented by the "Flag of Judah," are the tribes of Judah, Issachar, and Zebulun. To the south is the "Flag of Reuben," representing the tribes of Reuben, Shimon, and Gad. To the west is the "Flag of Ephraim," along with the tribes of Ephraim, Manasseh, and Benjamin. Finally, to the north is the "Flag of Dan," with the tribes of Dan, Asher, and Naftali.

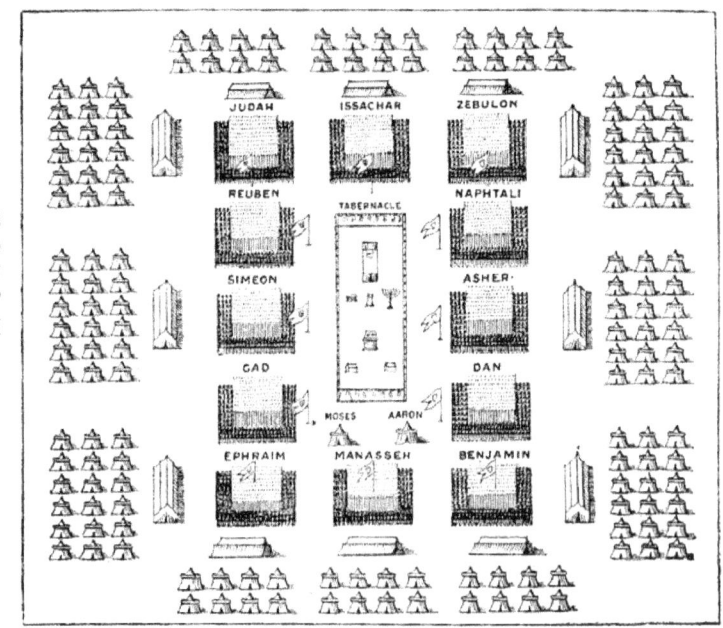

The Wilderness Camp, from a drawing in the *Biblia Sacra Polyglotta* (London, 1657).

BAMIDBAR (NUM 1:1—4:20)

Life Lessons from Bamidbar

From the name of the book, Numbers, you might think it's all about counting. It actually does start with a count, and the first life lesson we'll discuss comes from counting. But there is much more to the book, as we'll soon see.

Everyone is Special and Worth Counting

This week's reading, the very first of the book of Numbers, begins with God commanding Moses to count the Jewish people. (Counting people in a city or state or country is called a census, and in America, we do this every ten years.) This is not the first time God wants a census to be taken. In fact, it's the third census since the Jews left Egypt.

What's going on here with all this counting?

There is a famous midrash that answers this question with a parable (which is a story told to teach a lesson). The story describes a man who keeps his favorite treasures in a beautiful box. He loves these treasures so much that he often opens the box and takes them out. He looks at them. He holds them. And then he counts them, again and again, to be sure that they are all there.

Have you guessed the point of the story?

The Jewish people, says the midrash, are God's treasure, and He loves them so much that He, too, counts them again and again.

There is one other important point about these countings. If you look closely at each census, you will see that they are not done by counting people but by counting or listing the names of the people. Using names instead of numbers is another way God shows the Jewish people how dear they are to Him, since names are much more personal than numbers.

This is perhaps the simplest and most important life lesson we learn from Numbers. Each and every one of us is precious in the eyes of God. We are His treasures, and if we always remember that and keep it in mind before we act, we will surely do only those things that make God proud of us.

9

> *Your parents must certainly think of you as a treasure. What do you think makes you so special and dear to them? Do you think these things help make you special to God, too?*

Creating a Family Tree

In a sense, the beginning chapters of the book of Numbers are really one big family tree. Maybe you can use it as the inspiration for creating your own family tree.

You could start by interviewing your parents and asking them about their lives and their best memories. You could ask them to tell you stories about your grandparents and the lives they lived. You could gather up photos of yourself, your siblings and friends, your parents, grandparents, aunts and uncles, and so on.

You could even interview your grandparents and some of your aunts and uncles to see what they remember about your mom and dad. Maybe they'll have stories your parents have forgotten!

Once you have all these stories and photos, what comes next?

One way to organize and archive everything you've gathered is to use one of the online services designed to do just that. (One good and free example is https://www.ancestry.com/.) You will certainly need your parents' permission to do so, and probably their help, too. But in time, you will have your own book of numbers!

Good Individuals versus Good Communities

As we will see over the next several chapters, the book of Numbers is made up of stories about special individuals. Some of these people are very good, while others are less good. (Some are actually very bad people.) But each of these individuals is complicated. There are good people who make bad choices and end up doing bad things. And the bad people aren't completely bad. They actually have what we call "positive character traits."

Our challenge in studying these stories will be to distinguish the good from the bad. Obviously, we don't want to copy the bad

Bamidbar (Num 1:1—4:20)

things these people do. But we can and should learn from the good things that people do in these stories.

When we learn from the good things other people do, we call these people "role models." This is an idea we will talk about a lot in this book. People who are role models show us proper behavior. Being a role model can involve easy things, like always saying "please" and "thank you." Sometimes being a role model involves things that are harder to do, like giving to charity or volunteering our time. And sometimes, role models show us good character traits, such as always being honest or always being kind to others.

One of the interesting things about this week's reading is that, unlike much of Numbers, it has no stories about individuals. This week's reading focuses on the Jewish people as a whole, even going so far as to count them all! This focus on the community should cause us to ask an important but complicated question.

We will see in the rest of Numbers that the individuals who appear throughout the book have character traits that we should either learn from and copy or avoid. Again, that's what role models do: show us proper ways to act or highlight improper behavior that we should avoid. But what about an entire people? Can we talk about a people having certain character traits?

To answer this question, we need to turn to something called *anthropology*, which is the study of human societies and cultures and their development. People who work in this field are called *anthropologists*, and anthropologists have been trying to answer this question for quite some time. In doing so, they have looked closely at the people and cultures of many different countries. However, before looking at their findings, let's state something that should be obvious.

Not every person from a given country or people must or can be defined by "generalities." What makes something a "generality" is that it is often but not always observed. And, to be clear, these generalities do not stem from the nature of people. They are usually a product of the culture of a country. That is the point of the research anthropologists do: to discover or to show whether certain cultural traits or generalities are found in differing countries.

With this in mind, here is what research suggests.

American culture tends to produce people who are generally very self-confident and open-minded but can also be overly aggressive.[1] British culture is said to produce people who possess a quick and sharp sense of humor but can be distant and reserved, and British society has a strong focus on social standing and wealth.[2] The Germans, too, are frequently thought of as having a national character.[3] Mention German culture and the type of people it tends to produce, and certain traits quickly come to mind: direct, punctual, lovers of rules and structure.

Now that we have reached the twenty-first century, and China has increased its influence in the world, discussions of the Chinese people and their character traits have become more frequent and have been the subject of academic studies. And the findings? Chinese culture often produces individuals who are family oriented but at the same time often place the goals of the group as a whole over the needs and desires of each individual.[4]

It may seem that this focus on national character traits is new, perhaps even limited to modern times, but it is not. God Himself understood that the Jewish people have certain common traits, most notably that they are "a stiff-necked people" (Exod 32:9).[5]

So it seems that we can, in some sense, talk about a people having certain character traits. If so, can a people be a role model? From a Jewish perspective, the answer is yes, as the talmudic sages stated so simply and clearly: "Do not separate yourself from the community."[6] By this, these sages are saying that each individual ought to follow the example set by his or her community.

1. Terracciano and McCrae, "Perceptions."
2. McAlpine, "Lost in Translation."
3. Schäferhoff, "9 German Stereotypes."
4. Zhu, "A Comparative Look."
5. Various translations render the phrase "stiff-necked" (Sefaria, King James Version, and New International Version), as "stubborn and rebellious" (New Living Translation), and as "obstinate" (New American Standard Bible). Regardless of the translation, the sense is the same.
6. Pirkei Avot 2:4.

BAMIDBAR (NUM 1:1—4:20)

Communities have rules and standards that are meant to make its members better people. This is why Jewish communities have always had resources to help their members in times of trouble, such as charity funds and interest-free loan societies. There are committees to help families when someone is sick. Others help organize joyful events surrounding the birth of a baby or a marriage. And still others are there when someone dies and the family is in need of comforting.

In other words, a community that is defined by its good character can teach its members what it takes to be a good person and a productive member of society. It thus makes a great deal of sense for a book such as Numbers, which has so many stories about individuals, to begin by reminding us of the importance of people and community.

> *How would you describe the community you belong to? What good behaviors have you learned from this community?*

Naso

(Num 4:21—7:89)

Summary of This Week's Reading

This week's reading, Naso, is the longest single portion in the Torah, containing 176 verses. It starts with God informing Moses of the duties that two Levite families, Gershon and Merari, are responsible for transporting the tabernacle whenever the Jewish people travels through the Sinai wilderness. The Gershon family carried the tapestries, veils, and coverings of the mishkan, while the Merari family carried its structural components, such as the beams, boards, and pillars.

Our reading continues with a series of seemingly unrelated laws, but in truth, each is somehow connected to the mishkan. These include the law that certain individuals who become ritually impure may not enter the mishkan and its surrounding area, the sacrifice one must bring to the mishkan if one steals from another person and then lies about it, and the right of a person to give the various required priestly gifts to any priest of their liking.[1]

Next comes a long and difficult discussion of some very complicated laws. The first, called the law of the Sotah, involves a man who becomes unreasonably jealous of his wife and the special ceremony they undergo in the mishkan that either strengthens their marriage or leads to their divorce. The second, called the laws of the nazirite

---

1. These included things such as the firstborn of any domestic kosher animal and the first fruits of the harvest.

(nazir *in Hebrew) discusses a person who vows not to drink wine or eat any grape products. (We will discuss this in greater detail below). The reading concludes by describing the day when the mishkan is first officially used. The leaders of the twelve tribes bring special gifts for the occasion: six covered wagons and twelve oxen to be used to move the mishkan when the Jews travel. They also wanted to offer special gifts on behalf of their tribes, and while each leader brings his own gift, the gifts of these twelve men are identical. (We will talk more about this, too.)*

After we read about the tribal leaders and their gifts, we learn how God talks to Moses in the mishkan: Moses hears His voice coming from between the two cherubs atop the holy ark.

Life Lessons from Naso

At first glance, parashat Naso seems to be filled with complex and often boring laws with little relevance to our daily lives: instructions about carrying the mishkan in the Sinai wilderness; laws about a jealous husband and someone who won't drink wine; twelve identical gifts described twelve times. But the parasha has more to teach us if we take a closer look.

Bad Habits

If you were to ask your parents and teachers to list some bad or annoying habits, knuckle cracking would likely be toward the top of the list.

Many people think that cracking your knuckles is bad for you and can raise your risk of arthritis. According to the Harvard School of Medicine, that's simply not true. Cracking your knuckles may aggravate the people around you, but it probably won't do you any harm.[2] However, simply because it's not bad for you doesn't mean knuckle cracking is not a bad habit. Just ask the people who can't stand the sound of cracking knuckles.

---

2. https://www.health.harvard.edu/pain/does-knuckle-cracking-cause-arthritis.

Naso (Num 4:21—7:89)

Knuckle cracking, like any bad habit, is possible to break. It's just not so easy. It takes time, patience, and determination. It may also involve some gimmicks, like wearing a rubber band on your wrist and snapping it whenever you're about to crack your knuckles.[3] But this week's reading gives us another option when it comes to bad habits, and it's found in the story of the nazir.

A nazir is a person who vows not to drink wine or eat any grape products, which is a bit strange when you stop and think about it. Many adults drink wine with their meals or sometimes just to relax. What's more, a central part of the Jewish ritual for greeting the Sabbath on Friday evenings involves drinking a cup of wine. Why would anyone want to take a vow not to drink wine?

To answer this question, we need to step back and take a look at the story of Noah and the great flood found in the book of Genesis.

When the rains finally stop and the flood waters recede, Noah and his family are able to leave the ark, along with the many animals they have saved. One of the first things Noah does as he sets about rebuilding the world is plant a vineyard. Once the grapes are ready, he makes wine and drinks it. In fact, he drinks a lot of his wine, so much that he passes out in his tent.[4] His youngest son, Ham, discovers his father drunk and naked, but instead of respectfully covering up his father, he runs and tells his brothers (in a not-so-nice way) about their drunken father.

The rabbis of the Talmud see in this story a warning about the dangers of drinking too much wine. They describe the dangers, as they often do, through a parable. As they tell it, the satan slaughters a lamb, a lion, a monkey, and a pig over Noah's vineyard and proceeds to "water" the vineyard with their blood. The rabbis go on to explain the symbolism of each animal: a single drink makes a person as "meek" as a lamb; two drinks make one feel mighty as a

---

3. The online publication *Healthline* gives a number of tips to help break this habit in an article entitled "Is Cracking Your Knuckles Bad for You?" https://www.healthline.com/health/cracking-knuckles.

4. This story and some important life lessons to be learned from it are discussed at length in *A Curious Student's Guide to the Book of Genesis*.

lion; three or four drinks cause one to act like a monkey, "hopping about, dancing, giggling, and uttering bad words in public." More than that, and a person ends up wallowing in waste like a pig.

By now, you must be wondering, what does all this have to do with the nazir and bad habits? Here's the connection:

Let's assume that the nazir knows himself and his strengths and weaknesses. He knows how much he enjoys wine, and he is concerned that if he drinks wine, he won't know when to stop. From the story of Noah he certainly understands how bad a habit it is to drink too much wine. And so, the nazir takes a vow not to drink wine. In other words, instead of falling into a bad habit, he takes a positive step to avoid the habit completely.

It should be obvious to us that it is easier to avoid a bad habit than to break one. We shouldn't need the story of the nazir to remind us of this. But sometimes, we all need reminders, even about the most obvious of things, to get us back on the right track.

> *Ask your family to use the story of the nazir as an example and challenge everyone in your family to come up with a plan of action for breaking one bad habit. Then make a chart to track how long it takes each of you to do this.*

Intentions Matter—Or Do They?

Before we take a look at the gifts the leaders of each tribe bring on the first day the mishkan is put into use, it is worthwhile to go back and discuss the role these twelve men played in collecting all the materials needed to build the mishkan.

After the exodus from Egypt, when it was time to begin building the mishkan, Moses turned to the people. He told them that whoever wished should "bring an offering of the LORD." The people were so excited about having a mishkan that they gave and gave and gave, until Moses had to tell them to stop.

What about the princes, the leaders of the twelve tribes? What did they do? What did they give?

Naso (Num 4:21—7:89)

There is much debate about how the princes responded to Moses's request for "offerings of the LORD." One view says that their feelings were hurt because Moses turned to the people for offerings and not to them. And because their feelings were hurt, they stood back and didn't give anything. By the time they realized their mistake, it was too late. Moses had everything he needed to build the mishkan.

Another view says that they were very arrogant. According to this view, they were sure that the people would never be able to bring enough wood, fabric, gold, and silver to build the mishkan. The princes were sure that in the end, Moses and the people would have to turn to them to save the day. But the princes were wrong. The people gave more than enough to build the mishkan.

In the end, the princes understood the mistake they had made. While it was too late to contribute to the building of the mishkan itself, they brought materials to be used in making the priestly garments. Moses did not want to accept any contributions from the princes, and who could blame him? The princes had pouted, been arrogant, and stood back doing nothing when they, as leaders, should have been among the first to give. Then God Himself stepped forward and told Moses to accept the gifts of the princes.

What does God see that Moses doesn't? What is God trying to teach us by accepting the gifts Moses wanted to reject?

The lesson here is simple: When it comes to doing good deeds or observing God's commandments, intentions don't matter. What matters is what you do. For example, imagine that on Rosh Hashana, the Jewish New Year, your mom or dad blows a shofar just because you and the rest of the family enjoy the musical sounds it makes. Guess what? Even if your family doesn't intend to fulfill the commandment of sounding the shofar with this "musical concert," you still fulfill it. Think matzah is yummy? If you eat matzah on the first night of Passover, even if you're just eating because you like it, you still fulfill the biblical commandment.

The reverse is also true. If you say something mean to a friend and hurt his or her feelings, it doesn't matter that you didn't mean to hurt him or her. You still did. The same is true if you trip your little brother. Maybe you didn't mean for him to fall and skin his knee, but in the end, he has a skinned knee because of what you did.

It is commonly believed that Abraham Lincoln was the first to use the phrase "actions speak louder than words."[5] What is true of words is also true of intentions. It is your actions that count, no matter whether your intentions are good or bad.

> *Think back on a time when you unintentionally hurt someone. What did you do or say to try and make things right? How did your friend respond? What do you think might work better if it happens again?*

Difference is Important. So is Sameness.

Having discussed what the princes did (and didn't do) during the building phase of the mishkan, it is now time to take a closer look at what they did during the opening ceremonies for the mishkan.

As we have already mentioned, the princes collectively donate six carts and twelve oxen ("a cart for every two chieftains [leader of the tribe] and an ox for each one"). Moses divides these up among the Levites to be used in transporting the mishkan whenever the Jewish people travel in the Sinai wilderness.[6]

It is not surprising that the princes give gifts as a group. What comes next, however, is a bit unexpected: twelve separate but identical offerings from the princes. And what an offering it is: "one silver bowl weighing 130 shekels and one silver basin of 70 shekels by the sanctuary weight, both filled with choice flour with oil mixed in, for a meal offering; one gold ladle of 10 shekels, filled

---

5. In October 1859, Abraham Lincoln delivered what came to be known as the Cooper Union Address. In addition to uttering this now-famous phrase, he argued against allowing slavery to be introduced into territories that were not yet states and thus not yet part of the United States. As president during the Civil War, Lincoln eventually pushed not just for the restoration of the Union but for the abolishment of slavery, which came about with the passage and ratification of the Thirteenth Amendment in 1865.

6. Moses gave two carts and four oxen the Gershon family and four carts and eight oxen to the Merari family.

Naso (Num 4:21—7:89)

with incense; one bull of the herd, one ram, and one lamb in its first year, for a burnt offering; one goat for a sin offering; and for his sacrifice of well-being: two oxen, five rams, five he-goats, and five yearling lambs."

Two questions immediately come to mind. First, we know that each prince, when bringing his personal offering in addition to his tribe's communal offering, brings exactly what the other eleven princes bring. Why? Second, why does the Torah repeat the description of these offerings twelve times? Could it not have said something like "This is the offering that each of the twelve princes brought"?

In thinking about these questions, it is important to remember that each of the twelve tribes had a unique and special character. Jacob understood this when he blessed his twelve sons. Moses saw this when he blessed the twelve tribes. For instance, the members of the tribe of Reuben were known for their emotional swings and their fiery tempers. The tribe of Gad was cunning and resourceful. Zebulun was a tribe of sailors and successful businesspeople, whereas Issachar was made of up Torah scholars talented debaters. The people of Asher loved to cook and were very social. And the list of differences between the tribes goes on and on. More important, the tribes were proud of their differences and their unique traits. And so, we might have thought that each tribal leader would have brought an offering that reflected what made his tribe so special.

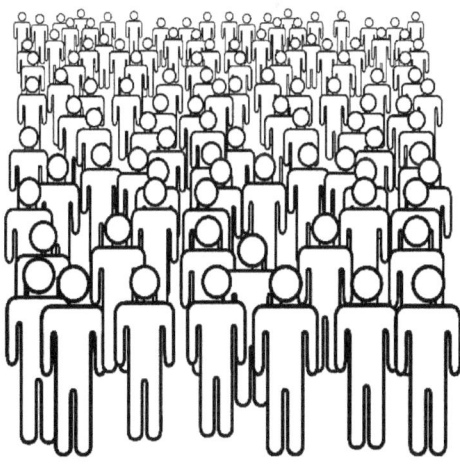

There is no doubt that the leaders understood how important each tribe's special traits were. But they also understood that when it comes to serving God by keeping His commandments and always trying to do good, we are all equal in His eyes. We are all equally dear to Him. And what better way to remind the people of this than by bringing twelve identical offerings to the mishkan?

For His part, God also wants to remind the Jewish people of this, and that is why the details of each leader's offering are repeated, even though it means that the same gifts are listed twelve times.

> *Does God really need our gifts? Of course not. So why do you think the princes wanted to give gifts to God? Do you ever wish that you could give gifts to God?*

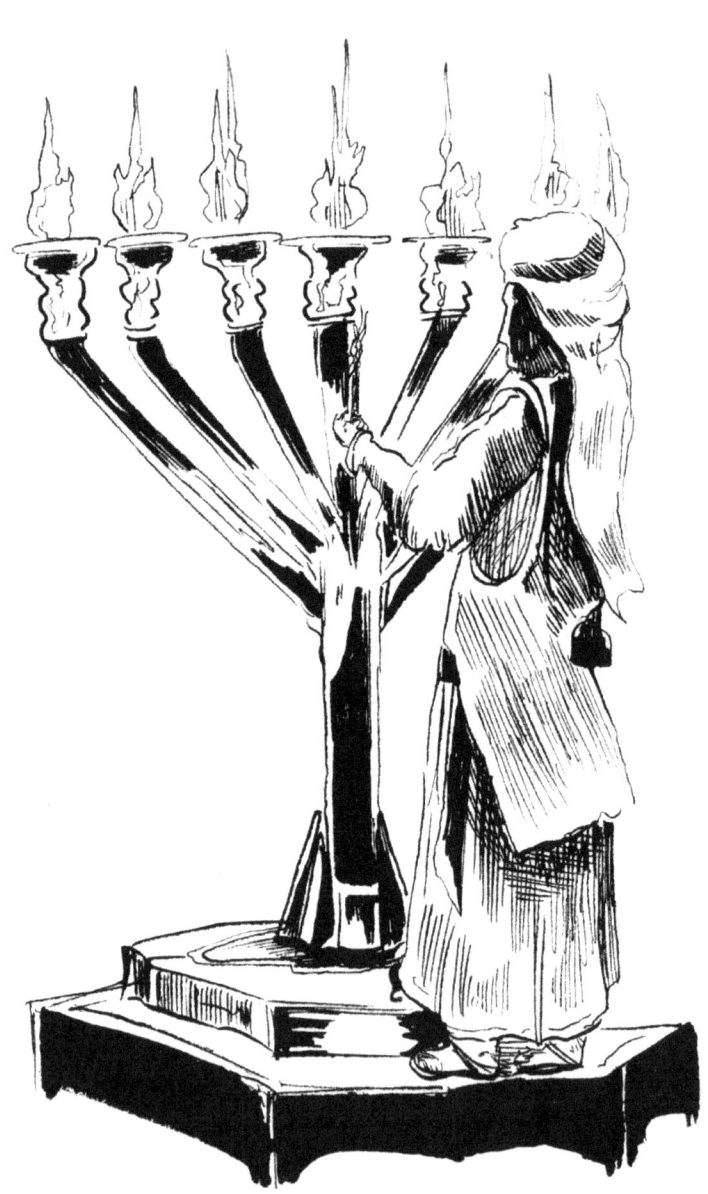

Beha'alotecha
(Num 8:1—12:16)

Summary of This Week's Reading

Our reading this week begins with God's command to Aaron to light the golden menorah that is found in the heart of the mishkan every day. God then tells Moses that it is time for the Levites to begin their work in the mishkan and what must be done so that they can begin this special work. Three steps are required: the Levites must shave their bodies, immerse in a ritual bathing pool (called a mikveh in Hebrew), and offer certain sacrifices. God also tells Moses that there are age requirements for the Levites. They are to begin their training at the age of twenty-five. At the age of thirty, after five years of training, their service begins, and they are allowed to work in the mishkan until the age of fifty. From age fifty on, they will serve as mentors and teachers to the younger Levites.

The text next relates a series of incidents related to the mishkan. For example, it was established upon the Jews' exodus from Egypt that the people were required to bring a special offering to celebrate the Passover holiday. We find in our reading that a group of individuals can't bring a Passover offering because they are ritually impure.[1] *They come before Moses and politely complain about being*

---

1. The Torah tells us (Num. 19:11) that anyone "who touches the corpse of any human being shall be *tamei* [ritually impure or, as some translate, unclean] for seven days." Touching, of course, includes carrying or moving a corpse even when it is in a coffin. And according to the midrash, this is exactly what these men have been doing. They have been carrying the coffins of Joseph and

excluded from the Passover offering. Moses shares their complaint with God, who responds by designating a "Second Passover." Anyone who cannot offer the Passover offering in its proper time can do so on the Second Passover, which comes exactly thirty days after Passover.

The text goes on to tell us that once erected, the mishkan is covered by a cloud during the day and a pillar of fire by night. When God wishes for the Jewish people to continue their travels in the wilderness, the cloud is lifted, and it leads the people through the wilderness. When it is time for them to stop, the cloud comes to rest.

How often does the cloud move? Sometimes the Jews stay only one night in a particular location before the cloud signals to them that it is again time to depart. There are other times when the Jews stay in one place for many years.

And why is this information in our reading this week? We see that nearly one year after the Jews arrived at Mount Sinai, the cloud rises from the mishkan, signaling that it is time to move on. The reading tells us how the mishkan is dismantled and how the people travel in the special formation described in the first of our Torah readings.

Sadly, this move does not go so well. Almost as soon as the people start traveling, they start complaining. First, they complain about how difficult the journey is. Then they grumble about the manna, saying that they want meat to eat. This causes Moses to tell God that he cannot lead this people any longer.

God, of course, responds to all this. He tells Moses to gather seventy elders who will assist him in his leadership duties. God then turns His attention to the people. He promises to provide the Jews with so much meat that "it will come out of their noses." How does God do this? He causes a wind to sweep in huge numbers of quail from the sea. The people gather piles of quail and start enjoying the meat of these birds. Those who eat and eat and eat and thus gorge themselves die in a plague.

Our reading concludes with the story of Miriam and Aaron discussing Moses's marriage to a "Cushite woman." We will discuss this story in detail later in this chapter.

---

his brothers out of Egypt so that they can be buried in the Holy Land. This is why they are ritually impure and are not allowed to bring a Passover offering.

Beha'alotecha (Num 8:1—12:16)

Life Lessons from Beha'alotecha

This week's reading features three very different stories, but each shares a common message: stuff matters. What kind of stuff, you may ask? Let's get started and see.

Perspective Matters

Sometimes we can learn from stories in the Torah just by looking at where they appear and how closely they follow other stories. This week's reading has one example of this.

Last week's reading, Naso, concluded by telling us in great detail of the offerings brought by each of the twelve princes of Israel. Aaron, of course, watched this, and while the text does not tell us what he was thinking, it's easy to imagine how he felt, at least according to the midrash. The midrash not only gives us insights into Aaron's thoughts and feelings, it also explains why the story of the princes comes right before the story that begins this week's reading: the command to Aaron to light the menorah every day.

Aaron is not only the High Priest, he is also the tribal leader of Levi, and the midrash[2] tells us how sad he felt watching all the other tribal leaders bring special gifts before God. He thought that

2. Midrash Tanchuma, Beha'alotecha 5.

27

perhaps he had done something wrong, and because of this, his tribe was not given a chance to bring special offerings along with the other tribes. In the midrash's version of this story, God understands Aaron's feelings, which is why He says to Moses: "Go, say unto Aaron, 'Do not be afraid. You are destined for something greater than this.'" And what is "this"? What is this greatness being promised to Aaron? It is the commandment to light the menorah that begins this week's reading.

How exactly is lighting the menorah greater than bringing a special offering in the mishkan? A simple answer is that those offerings were brought only once, when the mishkan was first put to use. Aaron's lighting the menorah was done twice daily, morning and evening. Aaron (and his sons after him) would continue to fulfill this commandment for hundreds of years, until the destruction of the Second Temple.

According to the midrash, God acknowledges this fact but then adds something else that is a little hard to understand: "The offerings [of the priests] remain in force as long as the temple exists, but the lamps [of the menorah lit by Aaron] are forever [as verse two states] 'in front of the menorah.'" With the destruction of the Second Temple in the year 70 CE, the menorah was lost forever. There would be no more light. So why does God comfort Aaron by telling him that the lamps are forever?

To answer this question, we need to think about light and what it symbolizes.

It seems that the starting point of the universe as we know it is light.[3] How do we know this? The creation story in Genesis de-

---

3. Individuals who favor a scientific explanation for the creation of the universe (as opposed to the creation story of Genesis) generally favor the "Big Bang" Theory. In brief, this theory says the universe started with an infinitely hot, infinitely dense singularity. This singularity, which scientists believe contained all the matter of the known universe, explored (a word that does not really capture what happened there) and then inflated over the next 13.8 billion years to the cosmos that we know today. Astronomers who study the stars and reflect on the origins of the universe use mathematical formulas and models to assist them in their research, but they also use equipment that can see the "echo" of the expansion through a phenomenon known as the cosmic microwave background. This phenomenon is sometimes called the "afterglow"

Beha'alotecha (Num 8:1—12:16)

scribes how the earth was "unformed and void, with darkness over the surface of the deep" when God begins the process of creation. Seeing this, God says, "Let there be light," and there was light. What's more, God Himself describes the light as good. He goes on to separate the light from the darkness. This explains (at least in part) why light is frequently used as a symbol of goodness, as we often see in movies and fairy tales and hear in children's stories. And this is perhaps what God is hinting at when He assures Aaron that the lamps are forever.

As long as the mishkan (and the two temples that came afterwards) were in existence, the wicks in the menorah were kept burning all day every day. Of course, the light was needed so that the priests who burned the incense or who brought the showbread into the holy of holies could see. But, as midrash suggests, the purpose of the menorah was more than simply to light up the space. God seems to be telling Aaron that the light of the menorah was no ordinary light. It was godly light, and as we read in Genesis, God's light is good, and it is always present. It is meant to help us see clearly, to see what is good in our lives and to steer clear of the bad.

With this insight, we now understand why God tells Aaron that "you are destined for something greater." Aaron is to bring God's light (which is filled with goodness) into the Temple, and from there, it will shine into the world. This leaves us with an important life lesson.

How you see things (what we call "perspective") is very important, and God's words to Aaron gave him a better perspective on the commandment to light the menorah.

At first, all Aaron could see were the crowds of people watching each prince bring a special offering to the mishkan. This went on for twelve straight days, and it seemed to Aaron much more important than lighting the menorah each day, which was done in the holy of holies, out of sight of the people. Then God reminds Aaron that his task is not a one-time thing but will continue for hundreds of years. God then gives Aaron a hint about the special and eternal

---

of the Big Bang. An afterglow is, of course, a form of light, and thus we see that scientists also believe that light was the starting point of our universe.

importance of light itself, namely, as the midrash puts it, Aaron's light and the goodness it represents will continue to shine long after the Temple itself has been destroyed And this changes Aaron's perspective and allows him to see the enduring significance of the commandment of lighting the menorah.

With the proper perspective, even something as simple as striking a match can be seen as a very important act.

> *Can you think of a time your perspective on something changed and you came to see it as more important than you first thought? What changed your perspective? How did your changed perspective make you feel?*

Appreciation Matters, Too

It's hard to find a person who doesn't like pizza. Some people like it so much that they would be happy to eat it every day.

Maybe you're one of those people. If so, let's imagine that your parents make your dreams come true. They let you eat pizza every day, but there's a catch. They don't give you slices of pizza. Instead, they give you pizza smoothies. They taste like pizza, but the experience of eating them is completely different. No holding it in your hand. No folding the slice in half. No enjoying its delicious aroma. Just drinking something that tastes like pizza.

Now let's imagine that all your parents give you to eat is pizza smoothies. Pizza smoothies, every day, day-in and day-out. No matter how much you might love the taste of pizza, it's easy to see how you might grow tired of pizza smoothies.

Perhaps you're thinking, What does pizza (or pizza smoothies) have to do with this week's reading? It's really rather simple, because one of the most important stories in this week's reading is about eating the same thing every day.

Throughout their forty-year journey in the Sinai wilderness, the Jewish people ate manna, which was a kind of miracle bread that fell from the heavens each morning. It is described as being "like coriander seed." (Coriander is an herb that today is said to

Beha'alotecha (Num 8:1–12:16)

have a tart lemon-lime taste.) Its color was "like bdellium."[4] (If you search online for bdellium, you will see that it is an orange-gold color.)

The text goes on to tell us that manna tasted "like rich cream." However, the midrash gives a much more striking description of its taste: "the (taste of the) manna changed for Israel into any taste that they desired, except for that of the five kinds." (The "five kinds" are the five foods the Jews mentioned in their complaint to God: cucumbers, melons, leeks, onions, and garlic.) This is, at least according to the midrash, what made the manna so miraculous. It would taste like anything you could imagine, even pizza (if pizza had existed back in those days!).

You might have thought that the people would have been thrilled with their bread from heaven, but they weren't.

> Then the Israelites wept and said, "If only we had meat to eat! We remember the fish that we used to eat free in Egypt, the cucumbers, the melons, the leeks, the onions, and the garlic. Now our gullets are shriveled. There is nothing at all! Nothing but this manna to look to!" (Num 11:4–6)

Crazy, right? Who wouldn't want a miracle food that could taste like anything you want? Well, let's not forget our discussion of pizza smoothies. A pizza smoothie might taste like the real thing, but it's not. So, too, with the manna. It could taste like pizza or a hamburger or any flavor of ice cream, but it still wouldn't be the real thing. Real food has more than taste. It has texture. It has a certain feel and smell, things that manna lacked.

Thinking about it this way makes the people's frustration with the manna a bit more understandable. Yet when God hears their complaints, God is very angry. Can you understand why? If not, look carefully again at their complaints. They cry. They complain bitterly. They even say that the food they ate in Egypt as slaves was better than the manna. Nowhere do they show any appreciation

---

4. You can even buy bdellium today. It is a resin that comes from certain trees in India and Ethiopia.

for this miracle food God created for them. And this is one of the very important lessons we find in the story of the manna.

Sometimes people complain for no good reason, and it's hard to take such complaints seriously. But even when people have a real reason to complain, they need to be thoughtful about how they express themselves. They need to be polite. They need to show gratitude when it should be shown. The Jewish people in the desert did none of these things. They instead said to God: "We want meat, and we want it now!"

Of course God was angry with them. And if you were to ever complain to your parents in such a manner, they would be angry with you, too.

> *If the Jewish people in this story were given a "do over," what would you tell them to say? How do you think they should have asked God for something different to eat? Now think about something you would like to change if given a "do over" and practice talking about it with your parent or teacher or even with a friend or a sibling.*

Avoiding Forbidden Speech Matters Most of All

There is a short, odd story toward the end of this week's reading. The story is introduced by the short verses: "Miriam and Aaron spoke against Moses because of the Cushite woman he had married: 'He married a Cushite woman!' They said, 'Has the LORD spoken only through Moses? Has He not spoken through us as well?'"

Many questions come to mind when reading these verses. Who is this Cushite woman? Why is she described this way? Is it a reference to her beauty, as some think? Is it a description of where she comes from, as others suggest?

While these are good and important questions, they are not the key aspect of the story. What matters most about the story is this: nothing Miriam and Aaron say about Moses is untrue, and yet, God is very unhappy with their conversation—so unhappy, in fact, that God strikes Miriam with a skin disease the Torah calls

Beha'alotecha (Num 8:1—12:16)

tzara'at,[5] which the text describes as "snow-white scales." What is going on here, and what are we to learn from the conclusion of this strange little story?

According to Jewish tradition, this story is all about the dangers of engaging in forbidden speech, or *lashon hara* in Hebrew. *Lashon hara* is a term you may have heard before but might not fully understand. *Lashon hara* is *any insulting or damaging statement spoken against or about another person.*

Many people mistakenly believe that something has to be false or a lie to be *lashon hara*. This is not the case. *Lashon hara* is anything that if publicized would cause a person physical or monetary harm or would cause him or her anguish or fear.

In other words, even truthful statements (like the ones Miriam and Aaron spoke) that hurt or embarrass another person would be considered *lashon hara*.

There is another important term you need to be familiar with if you are going to fully understand what lashon hara is: *rechilut*, which is often translated as "gossip." (Some English translations of the Torah translate it "talebearing.") *Rechilut* is going around telling stories (which are almost always embarrassing or meant to hurt another person) "just because."

There is a very important difference between *lashon hara* and *rechilut*. *Lashon hara* can sometimes be true. It may have been said with the best of intentions, but in the end, it hurts or embarrasses someone else. *Rechilut* always is said with the goal of hurting or embarrassing another person. It has no positive goal whatsoever.

---

5. Most English translations of the Bible translate this word as "leprosy." However, while scholars may not know exactly what *tzara'at* is, they generally agree that it is not leprosy.

Here is a simple summary of the laws of *lashon hara*, so that you can be aware of what it is and try to avoid it:

1. *How serious is* lashon hara?

    The sages in the Talmud discuss lashon hara at length and conclude that it is a terrible thing, worse even than the three cardinal sins of murder, immorality, and idolatry. These sages even say that one who regularly speaks *lashon hara* is like a person who denies the existence of God. And in response, God says, "I and he cannot live in the same world." (B. Arakhin 15b).

2. *Can I speak* lashon hara *so that I won't lose money?*

    The short answer is no. You may not engage in *lashon hara* even if keeping quiet means suffering a great financial loss and even if other people come to think of you as a "dummy" because you lost so much money.

3. *Can I speak* lashon hara *so that I won't be embarrassed?*

    Again, the short answer is no. You may not engage in *lashon hara* even if keeping quiet means that you yourself will be embarrassed. For example, let's imagine that you are with a group of friends working on a project in class. Instead of working on the project, they start speaking *lashon hara*

Beha'alotecha (Num 8:1—12:16)

about another classmate. You can't get up and leave because the teacher has said you must stay in your group. What do you do? It's kind of embarrassing to just sit there and not say anything. Doing that will make your friends think you're boring or not cool. But that is what you must do: sit there quietly and not join in their conversation. This is a hard one no matter how old or young you are.

4. *But what if it's true?*

    A truthful statement can still be *lashon hara* if spoken for no good reason. Let's try to think of an example of how this works in real life.

    Imagine that your bicycle broke, and you took it to Mr. Smith's Bike Shop to be repaired. It cost you lots of money to fix, and it never worked well because Mr. Smith is a terrible bike repair person. Can you go around telling your friends about Mr. Smith? No, you can't, because all you're doing is harming his reputation and possibly harming his business.

    Now, what if one of your friends came to you and said that her bike was broken and that she was looking for a good repair shop? She heard you used Mr. Smith to fix your bike, and she wanted your opinion. You can certainly tell her the truth about Mr. Smith (while being sure not to exaggerate), because by doing so you are helping her avoid the same problems you had.

5. *Are there any cases in which we can speak* lashon hara?

    Yes there are, but this requires great care.

    For example, you see Bobby harming Billy—maybe by breaking something of Billy's or by taking something of Billy's—and you aren't sure whether Billy knows what happened. Or maybe you see Bobby say something mean or embarrassing to Billy, and you know that Bobby never apologized. What can or should you do?

    In such a case, you may discuss the incident with others. Even though this might embarrass or shame Bobby, you may do so in order to help Bobby learn from his mistake and not do such things again.

It is important to understand that such cases are not always so clear-cut, and it would be best to discuss matters with your parents or maybe even one of your teachers before doing anything.

6. *Can we "take it back" if we speak lashon hara?*

Sadly, you can't. The truth is that the harm done by speech is even worse than the harm done by stealing or by cheating someone financially. This point is best illustrated by a well-known Chasidic tale:

A man went about the community telling hateful lies about the rabbi. Later, he realized the wrong he had done, and began to feel very sad about what it. He went to the rabbi and begged his forgiveness, saying that he would do anything he could to make amends. The rabbi told the man, "Take a feather pillow, cut it open, and scatter the feathers to the winds." The man thought this was a strange request, but it was a simple enough task, and he did it gladly. When he returned to tell the rabbi that he had done it, the rabbi said, "Now, go and gather the feathers. Because you can no more make amends for the damage your words have done than you can re-collect the feathers."

In the end, you can make up for the financial harm you cause another by either replacing a lost or broken item or paying for it. But, as this story teaches us, the harm done by speech can never be repaired, because, like the feathers in this story, you never know where your words will end up.

Shelach

(Num 13:1—15:41)

Summary of This Week's Reading

The Jewish people have left the region around Mount Sinai and are now at the border of Canaan, the land God promised to Abraham, Isaac, and Jacob. To help in their conquest of the land, God allows Moses to send spies to scout out the land. One member of every tribe—with the exception of the tribe of Levi—is chosen for this task. Moses instructs the scouts to bring back a report regarding the nature of the land, including its strengths and weaknesses. He also instructs them to bring back samples of the land's produce.

The spies spend forty days traveling throughout the land. When they return, they bring with them some fruit from the land—wonderful, extraordinarily large fruit—to show the people how wonderful the land truly is. But then they share a report about the land that is less than wonderful. They report that people living in Canaan are mighty and that their cities are well fortified and impossible to conquer. Only Caleb and Joshua, the scouts representing the tribes of Judah and Ephraim, disagree. These two men argue that the land is special, a land "flowing with milk and honey," just as God promised. They conclude by reminding the people that there is no reason for concern because God will surely bring them victory in battle.

Sadly, the Jewish people ignore Caleb and Joshua. They instead believe the other ten spies, and, as a result, spend that entire night *crying, saying that they would rather return to Egypt than be defeated in battle by the Canaanites.*

In the morning, God tells Moses that because the Jewish people lack faith in Him, He has decided to wipe them out in a massive plague. As he does time and again when the Jewish people sin, Moses prays to God. He tells God that killing the Jewish people will cause the other nations of the world to doubt God and to even mock God. Moses believes these nations will sarcastically say, "Oh, what a strong God. He could lead the Jews out of Egypt. But defeat the Canaanites? No way." Moses continues and says to God that these nations will assume that God lacks the power to defeat the Canaanites in battle, so instead, He slaughtered His people.

God hears Moses's prayer and shows mercy to His people. He will not destroy them, but they must be punished. The Jewish people will wander in the wilderness for forty years. What's more, during that time, all males over the age of twenty—with the exception of Joshua and Caleb—will die. Only the next generation will enter the promised land. As for the spies, God kills them right away with a plague.

When Moses tells all this to the Jewish people, they are sad. They are sorry, but it's too late. The punishment has been decided upon. But a group of people decides not to accept their punishment. They think they can "make amends" by entering Canaan and conquering it, as God originally told them to do. There is, however, a big problem with their plan. God does not approve of their actions, and when they try to invade Canaan, they are massacred by the Amalekites and Canaanites.

At this point, the story of the spies ends, and life in the wilderness continues, which is why our reading returns to the laws of the mishkan, specifically laws about how certain sacrifices must be brought with wine and a flour offering mixed with olive oil. We also read about how people must give a portion of the dough they prepare to the priests whenever they are baking bread for themselves.

The reading continues with laws that teach what must be done to a person who worships idols (whether inadvertently or intentionally) and to a person who intentionally violates the Sabbath.

Shelach (Num 13:1—15:41)

Finally, this week's reading discusses the commandment of putting tzitzit (fringes) on four-cornered garments, a topic we will discuss in greater detail below.

Life Lessons from Shelach

This week's reading marks an important turning point in the overall storyline of the book of Numbers as well as in the history of the Jewish people. It is thus not surprising that it contains some very important life lessons that continue to be relevant in our times.

The Problems with Thinking You Know Better

There are many stories in the Torah that are difficult to understand. One of the best known of these confusing stories is found in this week's reading, and it involves the spies that Moses sends to scout out the land of Canaan.

If you recall, the book of Numbers opens "on the first day of the second month, in the second year following the exodus from the land of Egypt." In other words, the Jewish people have only been in the desert a little more than a year when, in this week's reading, they reach Canaan, the land God promised to their ancestors. To prepare for their conquest of the land, the people ask Moses to send a group of men to spy out the land.[1] Moses agrees to their request and chooses twelve important men, each a leader

---

1. The story of the spies is told here in Numbers, in chapters 13 and 14. It is retold by Moses in the first chapter of the book of Deuteronomy. There are some notable differences between the two versions of the story, which it is beyond the scope of this book to discuss. For our purposes, it is worth noting that here, in Numbers, God instructs Moses to send out the spies. In Deuteronomy, when Moses is retelling the story, he states that the people came to him with a request to send spies. How do we explain this difference? Most commentators, including the midrash, maintain that the people did in fact ask Moses to send out spies. Moses then consulted with God, who tells him "to send (them) for yourself." In other words, the final decision was Moses's. The details of the mission itself, such as how many men to send and whom to send, were made by Moses "by the LORD's command."

of his tribe. This makes sense. Such an important mission requires skilled, knowledgeable leaders.

Moses gives the men very detailed instructions as to what to look for, and off they go, for forty days, to spy out the land. When they return, the spies share their report directly with the people. They begin their report in a very positive way: "We came to the land you sent us to; it does indeed flow with milk and honey." As they continue, though, the tone of their report changes, and the change can be traced to a single word: "but."

Yes, it is a beautiful land, they say, one that truly can be described as a land of milk and honey, but . . . the cities we saw are large and fortified. Plus, the people living in these cities are powerful and stronger than we are. In fact, they are so big that they looked like giants to us, and when we saw them, we realized that we must look like grasshoppers to them.

Such a negative report! What's worse, it is an untruthful report. Men as big as giants? A people who left Egypt with God's help, who became His chosen people and received His Torah—can such a people really be as insignificant and as unimportant as grasshoppers?

What were these spies whom Moses trusted, men who were leaders of their tribes, thinking? Were they not, as we see in this week's reading, "men of distinction" and all "heads of the children of Israel"? How could these great men give such a false report to the people?

In order to answer these questions, you need to be familiar with the expression *second-guessing*. When you second-guess something, you are questioning a decision that has already been made. For example, you order chocolate ice cream for dessert, but when it arrives, you think to yourself, I should have asked for vanilla. That is second-guessing.

Doing this to yourself is one thing, but when you second-guess other people's decisions, it is like saying to them, "I know better than you." It is as if you were telling them that your choice (or decision) would have been better than theirs. Of course, the

Shelach (Num 13:1—15:41)

worst form of second-guessing is to ignore what someone asks or tells you to do and then to instead do what you want to do.

This is exactly what the spies did, at least according to the midrash. They thought they knew better than God. Here's why:

As leaders, they felt themselves responsible for the well-being of the people, and somehow they thought that it would be better for the Jewish people to remain in the Sinai wilderness rather than enter the land of Canaan. Think about it. In the wilderness, they led a truly miraculous life. When they traveled, they were visibly directed by God Himself (by a column of smoke in the day and a pillar of fire at night). When they were thirsty, they drank from the well of Miriam, which accompanied them whenever and wherever they travelled. When they were hungry, they literally ate bread from heaven. From this perspective, who could blame the spies for wanting to remain in the wilderness? Theirs was a life of intense closeness to God. And so, thinking they knew better than God, the spies second-guessed God's decision. Entering Canaan, they thought, would distance the people from God, and who would want that?

Sadly, by telling such exaggerated lies to the people, the spies caused the entire nation to second-guess God as well. And as the story makes clear, neither the spies nor the people knew better than God. As a result of their second-guessing, the people lost the chance to enter into Canaan and take possession of it.[2]

> *Can you think of a time when you second-guessed your parents or one of your teachers? Why did you think you knew better than them? In the end, how did not doing what they asked of you work out?*

---

2. Ironically, the second-guessing did not end here. After crying and weeping all night long about God's decree, the people come to Moses in the morning and tell him: "We are prepared to go up to the place that the LORD has spoken of, for we were wrong." Moses tells them that it is too late to change their minds. God has decreed against them. But again, the people ignore Moses and God and try to invade the land of Canaan on their own. Their invasion fails miserably, and they suffer a crushing defeat at the hands of the "Amalekites and the Canaanites who dwelt in that hill country."

Intentions Don't Matter. Actions Do.

There is another important lesson to be learned from the story of the spies. It involves answering a simple question, What matters more? Your intentions or your actions? We considered this question back in the chapter on Naso, but it is important enough to be worth revisiting.

As we have explained the story of the spies (and in fairness, there are a number of different ways to explain this story), the spies had good intentions. They were convinced that it would be better for the Jewish people to remain in the wilderness than to enter into the land of Canaan. Their convictions drove them to mislead to the Jewish people about the land and the people who lived there.

Unfortunately, the people believed their lies and exaggerations. They wept all night long thinking about the report the spies brought back. In the morning, they lashed out against Moses and against God. They cried out: "If only we had died in the land of Egypt, or if only we might die in this wilderness! Why is the LORD taking us to that land to fall by the sword?" They even went so far as to say that it would be better for them to go back to Egypt. Some even proposed the idea of turning around and actually going back to Egypt.

As you could well imagine, God isn't too pleased with the people's reaction. He is angry—so angry that He is ready to strike down the people with a plague and disown them. Moses prays for the people, and God hears his prayers. He does not wipe out the people, but their fates are sealed. God decrees that the people spend forty years wandering in the wilderness. What's more, any man who is twenty years or older at this time will die in the wilderness and never see the promised land.[3]

The spies may have had the best of intentions, but their action led to a disastrous outcome for the Jewish people. And the

---

3. There were two exceptions to this decree. Joshua and Caleb, who were among the spies but who tried to counter the lies of the other ten spies, were allowed to live and enter the land. Moses, as we will discuss later in this book, was not allowed to enter the land for reasons having nothing to do with this story, but God showed it to him before his death.

outcome was disastrous for them, too, because after pronouncing His decree against the nation, God struck down these ten men, and "they died of plague, by the will of the LORD."

You have probably heard friends say "I didn't mean it" when they were caught doing something wrong or inappropriate. Maybe you've said this, too. But the story of the spies comes to teach us that intentions (good or bad) don't count for much when compared to actions. In the end, what you actually do counts far more than what you intended to do.

> *Think of a time when you said "I didn't mean it" to your parents or to a friend. Why do you think you said that? Were you afraid to tell the truth? Did you think you wouldn't get into trouble because you "didn't mean it"? What eventually happened?*

The Power of Visual Reminders

Have you ever thought about your learning style, that is, what helps you to best learn and remember new information or facts? Are you one who learns by doing? Do you have to hear things to fully grasp and remember them? Or do you need to see things to learn the material well?

The idea that different students have different ways of learning is well-known to both teachers and researchers. Yet there is general agreement that everyone can benefit from visual cues and visual reminders, regardless of his or her learning style.

You probably have a bunch of different posters hanging up in your classroom. For young children, these may be posters of colors or basic math facts or even classroom rules. As children grow older, the topics of the posters may change and become more complicated, but their purpose remains the same: to help students remember key information necessary to help them succeed in school.

Adults, including your parents, also rely on visual reminders. From notes left on refrigerator doors to pop-up alerts on cell phones, moms and dads all over the world rely on visual reminders to keep their homes running smoothly and to get their children where they need to be when they need to be there.

Even countries rely on visual reminders to represent things their country stands for. America has always stood for freedom, and perhaps there is no better visual reminder of this than the Statue of Liberty.

Of course, Judaism has its own set of visual reminders. Perhaps you are familiar with some of them, like the mezuzah that is put on the doorposts of virtually every Jewish home.[4] The mezuzah reminds a family that their home should be a place where God is welcome and where He is a part of the family's life. The candles that many Jewish families light on Friday nights are another important visual reminder. They are there to remind parents and children alike about

---

4. The Hebrew word *mezuzah* means "doorpost." According to the biblical commandment, a mezuzah is to be placed on all doorposts in a Jewish home, from the front door to the doors of each interior room (except for bathrooms). The mezuzah itself consists of a small scroll of parchment on which are written two biblical passages, Deuteronomy 6:4–9 and Deuteronomy 11:13–21, respectively.

Shelach (Num 13:1—15:41)

the importance of the Sabbath and how they can make the Sabbath a special day for the entire family.

If you haven't guessed by now, a very important part of this week's reading has to do with another of Judaism's visual reminders: tzitzit.

At the end of this week's reading, God commands the Jewish people to put fringes (*tzitzit* in Hebrew) on the corner of their garments. God makes clear why He gives them this commandment: "[You shall] look at it and recall all the commandments of the LORD and observe them." In other words, these fringes are to be a visual reminder to the Jewish people about God's laws and the importance of observing them.

Many ask, Why is this commandment given in this week's reading? What does it have to do with the story of the spies, which is the key part of this week's reading? The most common answer is that tzitzit are an appropriate way for the Jewish people to make amends for the sin of the spies. Simply put, the spies followed their eyes, not their hearts. The spies believed what they saw—a land populated by giants too strong for the Jewish people to overcome—rather than what they knew to be true: that the God who redeemed them from Egypt would help them conquer the land of Canaan. This explains why the commandment of tzitzit states that they are to be worn "so that you do not follow your heart and eyes in your lustful urge."

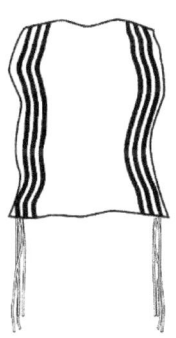

47

This is not to say that wearing tzitzit always keeps people from doing the wrong thing or ignoring God's commandments. But the Jewish people have long understood the reason for wearing tzitzit, and they gladly embraced this commandment. It was easy to fulfill this commandment when the Jewish people were wandering in the Sinai wilderness, because the custom at that time was for men to wear robe-like garments with four corners. (These garments were similar to what we today call ponchos.) Over time, clothing changed, and men no longer wore garments with four corners. Yet Jewish men weren't willing to give up their beloved tzitzit, and so a new custom developed of wearing a small four-cornered garment, called a *tallit katan* or simply *tzitzit*, under one's regular clothes in order to preserve the commandment.[5] To this day, many Jewish men wear these small garments every day.[6]

The garment that today is called *tzitzit* may be small, but the idea is not. Visual reminders such as tzitzit are powerful tools for helping us stay true to God's laws.

What do you think is the best visual reminder you rely on? Why does it work for you?

---

5. There is a separate custom of wearing a tallit gadol, or a prayer shawl, when attending services in a synagogue or even when praying at home. In non-Orthodox synagogues, these prayer shawls are worn by men and women.

6. For a variety of reasons, these small garments, which are simply called *tzitzit*, are typically worn by men. However, there is nothing in Jewish law that forbids women from wearing them, too, and some women do.

Korach

(Num 16:1—18:32)

Summary of This Week's Reading

This week's reading centers on the rebellion Korah stages against Moses and Aaron. Together with a few other ringleaders, Korah gathers 250 great and important men and accuses Moses and Aaron of keeping the power that comes from being leaders all to themselves. They are particularly annoyed that Aaron has been made high priest.

    When he hears their complaints, Moses proposes a test for the following day, one that will prove who is really worthy of being high priest. Everyone is to bring an incense offering to the mishkan, and God will then reveal to the people His choice for high priest. But Moses knows deep down that this test is a bad idea and that God has already selected Aaron as high priest. He therefore tries his best to convince Korah and his followers not to take part in the test. They ignore Moses's advice and insist on the test. In response, Moses pleads with God not to accept the incense offerings of the rebellious group.

    The night before the test, Korah walks through the camp trying to rile up the people against Moses. In the morning, he gathers them all at the entrance of the mishkan to witness the test.

    God's glory appears, and He is angry with those who have joined with Korah. God is so angry that He considers destroying all the Jews! Moses and Aaron pray to God to spare the people, and He agrees. But He still punishes Korah and his 250 rebels. The earth opens up and swallows Korah and his family, and a heavenly fire consumes the rest of the 250 rebels.

Moses tells Aaron's son Elazar to gather up the frying pans that were used for the incense offering, flatten them, and then use them to cover the incense altar. (This will be a visible reminder to never again challenge Aaron's role as high priest.)

The next day, the community complains loudly. They believe that Moses and Aaron are responsible for the deaths of "God's people." This, too, angers God. He tells Moses and Aaron to step aside so that He can destroy the complainers, and that is exactly what He does. Many thousands are struck down by a plague. But Moses, ever ready to protect and defend the Jewish people, tells Aaron to take a firepan with incense and go among the dying people. The burning incense, Moses says, will atone for their sin. Aaron does so, and the plague comes to an end.

Still, there remains the challenge to the choice of Aaron as high priest. God tells Moses to take a staff from an almond tree for each of the tribes.[1] On each staff is written the name of the tribe's prince. There is a thirteenth staff to represent the tribe of Levi, and Aaron's name is on that staff. The staffs are placed in the holy of holies chamber of the mishkan, where they remain until morning. When they are removed, Aaron's staff has miraculously budded with almond blossoms and almonds.

Here is the definitive proof that Aaron is God's choice for high priest, and God commands Moses to return "Aaron's staff" to the holy of holies, where it is to remain forever.

After seeing some of their fellow Jews swallowed by the earth or killed in a plague, it is understandable that many among the Jewish people are now afraid that they, too, might die if they enter a restricted area of the mishkan by mistake. To reassure them, God instructs the priests and the Levites to carefully guard the mishkan to prevent non-priests from entering without permission.

While on the topic of the mishkan, our reading goes on to list the various gifts the priests are entitled to. These include the privilege

---

1. For this test, the tribe of Joseph is represented by the tribes of Ephraim and Menashe, which brings the total number of staffs to twelve.

Korach (Num 16:1—18:32)

of eating certain sacrifices as well as select portions of other sacrifices; receiving the five shekels for the redemption of Israelite firstborn sons; a portion of all grain, oil, and wine crops; the "first fruit"; and more. As for Aaron, he is told that his descendants will not get a portion in the land of Israel. Instead, God will be their inheritance and portion.

The Levites are also told that they will not receive a share of the land of Israel. Instead, they are entitled to a tenth of all the Israelites' crops. This is a form of repayment for the services they now perform in the mishkan (and for the services they will in the future perform in the temple). But the Levites, like all the other Jews, must in turn give a tenth of what they receive to the priests.

Life Lessons from Korach

In this week's reading, we find yet another story that ends badly for the Jewish people, and, as with the previous sad stories we have read, this one has several very important life lessons for us.

Jealousy Removes a Person From This World

The first and most obvious question we need to ask about Korah's rebellion is this: What is it really about? What really drives Korah to rebel against Moses's leadership?

A simple reading of the text seems to give us an answer. Korah believes that each and every Jew is holy, as he says quite clearly to Moses: "All the community are holy, all of them, and the LORD is in their midst." In other words, Korah is saying to Moses, Why do we need you to stand before God and bring the word of God to the people? God already spoke to the entire Jewish nation at Mount Sinai. He can surely do it again any time He wishes.

You might think this puts an end to our question. The problem is, the rabbis who compiled the midrash never limited themselves to a simple reading of the text. They note that the story of Korah's rebellion starts with some unusual language: "Now Korah, son of Izhar son of Kohath son of Levi, took himself." What does "took himself" mean?

One explanation found in the midrash is that Korah took himself—that is, separated himself—from the community. Why would he do this? Because, says the midrash, he was jealous of Moses.

To understand Korah's jealousy, we need to take a look at his family tree. It seems that Korah and Moses were first cousins, which means that their fathers were brothers, with Moses's father Amram being the oldest of the brothers. The table below, which is based on chapter six of Exodus, explains their family ties.

Father (in birth order)	Children (in birth order)
Amram	Miriam, Aaron, and Moses
Izhar	Korah, Nepheg, and Zichri.
Hebron	None listed in the Torah
Uzziel	Mishael, Elzaphan, and Sithri.

The sons of Kohath [who was the son of Levi]: Amram, Izhar, Hebron, and Uzziel; and the span of Kohath's life was 133 years.

In those times, the first-born male child was automatically the leader of the family or the tribe. Moses's father, himself a great man, was not only the leader of the tribe of Levi but of the Jewish people while they were in Egypt. Korah knows and understands this. He accepts it, and so, when Moses became leader of the people, having been selected by God Himself, Korah accepted this, too. It made sense for the son of a first-born like Amram to be leader, even if this son, Moses, was not a first-born himself.

However, there are other important jobs besides being the leader of the people, and Korah thinks that he, as the first-born of Kohath's second son, Izhar, is entitled to one of these positions. The most important of these other jobs is that of high priest, and this is the job Korah wants. This is the job he thinks he deserves. But God had other ideas, and He picked Aaron to be the high priest.

Korach (Num 16:1—18:32)

"What?" thinks Korah. "Two sons from one family get the two best jobs!" (It doesn't matter to Korah that God chose Moses and Aaron for their jobs.)

Korah is angry. He is jealous. He feels cheated, and he feels even more cheated when Moses (as commanded by God) names Elzaphan to be leader of the Kohath family. (This family was responsible for all the utensils used in the mishkan.) To him, this makes no sense at all. "I am Izhar's son. I deserve to be leader of the Kohath family," cries Korah. "Should the youngest of my father's brothers become superior to me?"

Unwilling to accept any of this, Korah leads a rebellion against Moses and Aaron, which ends with Korah and his followers being swallowed up by the earth in a miraculous manner.[2] Soon afterwards, "a fire went forth from the LORD and consumed the two hundred and fifty men offering the incense." Truly a sad ending to a sad story.

From a Jewish perspective, it is not at all surprising that a story driven by jealousy has such a bad ending.

The talmudic rabbis are very clear about the evils of jealousy: "Jealousy, lust, and the [pursuit of] honor remove a person from the world" (Avot 4:21).[3] What's more, these rabbis understood

---

2. The verses (Num 28–32) tell us exactly why Korah and his followers died in such an unusual way: "And Moses said, 'By this you shall know that it was the LORD who sent me to do all these things; that they are not of my own devising: if these men die as all men do, if their lot be the common fate of all mankind, it was not the LORD who sent me. But if the LORD brings about something unheard-of, so that the ground opens its mouth and swallows them up with all that belongs to them, and they go down alive into Sheol, you shall know that these men have spurned the LORD.' Scarcely had he finished speaking all these words when the ground under them burst asunder, and the earth opened its mouth and swallowed them up with their households, all Korah's people and all their possessions."

3. Phrases like "remove a person from the world" can be hard to understand. Here are two ways to think about it. Jealousy and chasing after honor can separate a person from friends and family, which, in a sense, removes a person from important relationships that can define a person's "world." These actions can also make it seem like a person doubts God's ability to control the world or questions God's decisions as to how the world should run. When a person thinks, I should have that honor instead of another, it's like saying to

55

that jealousy can make a person resent the good fortune that comes to others, just like Korah resented the honor Moses and Aaron received. One of these rabbis was so concerned about the dangers that go along with being jealous that he would pray every day: "May it be acceptable before You, O LORD my God and God of my fathers, that no envy of us enter the heart of any man, nor the envy of any man enter our heart" (Y. Berakhot 7d).

While we may not pray daily to be spared from jealousy, perhaps we should on a daily basis remember this story of Korah and the very great dangers of being jealous and of letting that jealousy control our thoughts and actions.

> *The Jewish sages in Pirkei Avot ask, "Who is rich? One who is happy with their lot." In other words, a person cannot be happy or content if he or she is jealous of others. Are you content with what you have? Do you sometimes feel jealous of your friends or your siblings? What do you do when you have these feelings?*

The Dangers of Bad Neighbors

As we saw in the summary of this week's reading, Korah did not act alone in his rebellion against Moses. The first to join him were two men named Dathan and Abiram, and while this is the first time they are mentioned by name, it is not, at least according to the midrash, the first time they cause problems for the Jewish people.

According to the midrash, Dathan and Abiram watched over Jewish slaves in Egypt in order to keep track of how much work the slaves did each day. If the slaves didn't do enough work, they were beaten by Dathan and Abiram's Egyptian bosses. How awful!

There's more. If you recall, when Moses first went out to meet his real people, he saw an Egyptian taskmaster beating a Jewish slave. Moses was so outraged by this that he killed the Egyptian and hid his body in the sand along the Nile River. Moses thought

---

God, "God, you made the wrong choice." This kind of attitude can damage a person's relationship with God and thus remove the person from the "spiritual world."

Korach (Num 16:1—18:32)

he had hidden his crime, but the midrash explains that Dathan and Abiram reported him to Pharaoh. Moses, as we know, had to flee for his life.

The midrash gives many more examples of the trouble Dathan and Abiram caused, and so it is no surprise that they join Korah's rebellion. They are seen as troublemakers through and through. But what is surprising is that 250 men from the tribe of Reuben also join forces with Korah.

What's going on?

As we discussed in the first chapter of this book, when the Jews camped in the desert, there was a very specific order they followed in setting up their camp.[4] Each of the twelve tribes had its own special spot. The place of the tribe of Reuben was in the south of the camp. And who were their neighbors? Kohath and his sons, which means that the men from Reuben heard Korah's complaints firsthand, and they heard them over and over. Ultimately, they adopted Korah's complaints as their own.

The rabbis of the Talmud read this story and explained: "Woe to the wicked, woe to his neighbor!" They understood that we all tend to be influenced by the people we hang out with. When we are with good people who set good examples, it is easy to follow those examples. And if we hang out with complainers or troublemakers? How long will it be before we, too, become complainers and troublemakers? Looking at the story of Korah, not very long at all.

> *Can you think of a time you did something you weren't supposed to do just because your friends were doing it? Did you realize at the time that you were doing something wrong? Did you understand afterward that it would have been better not to follow their example? Why?*

---

4. See the summary at the end of chapter one for an illustration showing how the camp was set up.

For the Sake of Heaven

We discussed how Korah's complaints against Moses seem reasonable at first. The fact that God spoke to all the Jewish people at Mount Sinai proves that they are all holy. Korah therefore asks, What need is there for you, Moses, to represent us before God? However, Korah's argument against Moses is weakened by the debate he has with Moses and, according to the midrash, by the fact that he mocks Moses.

In an effort to make Moses look silly in the eyes of the people, Korah asks Moses two questions. The first has to do with a house that is filled with copies of the Torah and other holy books. Does this house need a mezuzah?

"Of course," says Moses, "God commanded that every Jewish home have a mezuah on its doorpost."

"Really?" Korah answers back. "Does a house full of holy books really need a mezuzah to remind the people who live there about God and His commandments? That's just silly!"

The second question is about an article of clothing that is made entirely of *techelet* (wool dyed a certain shade of blue). Does

Korach (Num 16:1—18:32)

it still need to have a string of *techelet*, that is, of blue-dyed wool, in the fringes (*tzitzit*) tied to each corner of the garment?

"Of course," says Moses, "God commanded that every four-cornered garment have a string of techailet on each corner."

"Really?" Korah answers back. "Must one really tie a little blue string of techailet to each corner if the entire garment is made of blue-dyed wool? That's even sillier!"

The tone of these questions and of Korah's responses to Moses show that he isn't serious in his complaints. He isn't interested in a serious discussion or debate with Moses. He is looking to argue and fight with him, and Jewish teachers and sages use this story to make an important point. Fighting among ourselves is bad. It leads to bad things. Friends stop speaking to one another when they fight. Countries sometimes go to war when their fights become too big and too bad. The Second Temple, the rabbis teach us, was destroyed because the Jews living in Jerusalem at that time hated each other for no good reason (something called *sinat chinam* in Hebrew) and were therefore always fighting among themselves.

Does this mean that you can never disagree with your siblings or with your friends? No, it doesn't. But what it does mean is that we must be careful to see the difference between a disagreement or a dispute and a fight. The rabbis of the Talmud explained it this way: When people disagree for good reasons and with the goal of making things better, they will find ways to agree and to compromise. There will be a positive outcome. The rabbis called this "a dispute that is for the sake of Heaven."

When people argue and fight for bad reasons or for no good reason at all, they are unlikely to agree on anything. Each will want things done his or her way. This, the rabbis said, is a dispute "not for the sake of Heaven."[5]

---

5. The phrase "for the sake of Heaven" appears frequently in the rabbinic literature, but it can be hard to define. Perhaps the best way to think of it is acting sincerely to try to fulfill God's will. And how do we know God's will? A good place to look (or at the very least to start looking) is God's law as set forth in the Torah and its commandments. There we are given some very specific instructions about how to act and what is expected of us. There is one other aspect to acting "for the sake of Heaven," and that is, you act for God's sake,

To help us understand the difference, the rabbis gave us an example of each: "Which is the controversy [or argument] that is for the sake of Heaven? Such was the controversy of Hillel and Shammai. And which is the controversy [or argument] that is not for the sake of Heaven? Such was the controversy of Korah and all his congregation.[6]

Hillel and Shammai were two of the greatest scholars in Jewish history. They (and their students after them) had many debates and disagreements about Jewish law. But their disagreements never became personal. Hillel and Shammai respected each other greatly. And even when they disagreed about certain points of Jewish law, they considered each other's arguments carefully. They were never rude to each other. They never thought the other's opinions were silly. The goal of both of them was to help the Jewish people better understand God's commandments, and this is why theirs was a "controversy that is for the sake of Heaven."

This was certainly not true for Korah. He was jealous of Moses. He mocked Moses. He led a rebellion against Moses. Of course, his controversy, which was "not for the sake of Heaven," did not endure (that is, last for a long time). Neither did Korah.

> *How can you tell when you are disagreeing with your friends or fighting with your siblings? Is it a question of how loud you are? Does it depend on the words you use? Does it come down to whether you want to find a way to agree or whether you simply want to win the argument?*

---

not your own. In other words, you try to fulfill God's will not because it will impress people or make them think highly of you, but instead because you are simply trying to carry out the word of God as best you can.

6. Pirkei Avot 5:17 .

Chukat

(Num 19:1—22:1)

Summary of This Week's Reading

Our reading this week begins with a difficult and mysterious commandment: the laws regarding the red heifer. We will skip over these laws right now, but we will discuss them in detail a little later in this chapter.

We next read about the death of Moses's sister Miriam, which occurs in the fortieth year of the Jews' wanderings in the Sinai wilderness. When Miriam dies, the well that miraculously provided the people with water throughout their travels dries up. Not surprisingly, the people become fearful and agitated and complain bitterly to Moses about the lack of water. This, too, is a difficult and complicated story. (Spoiler alert: It does not have a happy ending.) We will discuss this story in great depth as part of the life lessons that follow.

When the story about the lack of water comes to an end, Moses sends messengers to the king of Edom asking permission to pass through his land (which is south of Canaan). Passing through Edom would make the journey to Canaan much shorter. Moses promises the king that the Jewish people will not harm his land while passing through, but the king still will not agree to Moses's request. The Jews must therefore travel around the land of Edom and approach Canaan from the east instead of the south.

As they continue their travels, the Jewish people arrive at Mount Hor. At God's command, Moses, Aaron, and Aaron's son Elazar go up the mountain. Aaron removes the special clothing he wears as high priest and hands it over to his son Elazar. Aaron then passes away. The entire nation mourns Aaron's death for thirty days.

Soon thereafter, the Amalekites, disguised as Canaanites, attack the Jews. The Jews pray to God, and with His help, the Jews are victorious.

We next read about the people complaining once again about the manna. They say they are "disgusted" by it. God does not appreciate their lack of gratitude, and so He sends serpents into their camp. Many Jews die from the bites of these serpents. Realizing their mistake, the people turn to Moses and beg him to pray to God on their behalf. This Moses does. And how does God answer Moses's prayer? He tells him to make a serpent of copper and then to place it on top of a long pole. Those who look up at the copper serpent will be saved.

It is worth noting something obvious here. It is not the copper serpent that cures the people. As the talmudic rabbis explain: "Could a snake [on a pole] cause death [by not looking at it] or give life [by looking at it]? Rather, when Israel would look upward and subject their hearts to their Father in Heaven, they would be cured; but if not, they would waste away."[1]

Back to the stories found in this week's reading.

The Jews continue their journey, making their way toward the eastern bank of the Jordan River. At this point, the story of their travels is interrupted with a strange reference to "the Book of the Wars of the LORD." This seems to be a book that described all the battles the Jewish people fought in the wilderness and all the miracles God did to help them in those battles. One of the battles is hinted at in our reading this week. It seems that the Amorites were hiding in the Arnon valley waiting to ambush the Jewish people. Without giving us details, the text makes clear that God performs a miracle and wipes out the hidden army in order to save the Jewish people. The Jews do not know exactly what God did, but they know that He saved them. They therefore sing a song of praise to Him.

Following this, the Jews approach the land of the Amorites (which lies on the east bank of the Jordan River.) They send a

1. B. Rosh Hashana 29a.

Chukat (Num 19:1—22:1)

message to Sichon, king of the Amorites, asking permission to pass through his land on their way to Canaan. Just like the king of Edom, Sichon says no to their request. He masses his armies and attacks the Jews. Not surprisingly, the Jews are victorious. (After all, God is on their side.) Next up is Og, king of Bashan. He also attacks the Jews, and he and his armies also go down in defeat, only this time, the defeated king is killed.

The reading ends with the Jewish people at bank of the Jordan River, just across from the city of Jericho in the land of Israel.

Life Lessons from Chukat

This week's reading has some stories that are hard to understand, and they often leave readers with unanswered questions. But, as we know, this is no reason for us not to keep asking our questions. Whether our questions are answered or not, there are a number of important life lessons to be learned from these stories.

That Makes No Sense!

Imagine that your parents buy you a beautiful winter coat. You're outside playing. It's been raining, and maybe even some snow has fallen. Try as you might, you can't help but get your new beautiful coat dirty. When you show it to your parents, they say to you: "No worries. Just go back outside and jump in the biggest mud puddle you can find. That will take care of it."

Does that make any sense to you? Certainly not, but in a way, that is exactly what's going on in this week's reading with the laws of the red heifer. (A heifer is a young female cow that has not borne a calf.)

To understand this comparison, you need to know a bit more about how the mishkan worked (and this was also true centuries later when the temple was built to replace the mishkan). As you might imagine, people who came to the mishkan to offer sacrifices wanted to look their best, which probably meant they were freshly bathed and wearing their best clothing. After all, they were about to enter God's house, to stand in His presence and to offer Him gifts.

But there was more to getting ready to enter the mishkan than being physically clean. A person had to be "ritually clean," too. Ritual cleanliness was not something you could see. Instead, it meant staying away from certain things that the Torah describes as being "impure." These included animals like snakes and rats or animals that died in the field (or were killed by other wild animals). These were things that a person could easily come into contact with in those times.

There was one other important source of ritual impurity—the biggest source actually: a dead human body. Generally speaking, people do not come into contact with dead bodies. But it does sometimes happen in the normal course of daily life. Going to a funeral or visiting a cemetery is considered coming into contact with a dead body. Doctors who treat very sick patients, some of whom don't survive, come into contact with dead bodies. At times, so do soldiers or, sadly, police officers and fire fighters.

Ritual impurity is hard for us to fully understand because without a mishkan or a temple, we don't worry about it. It has no practical meaning in our times. But for the Jewish people wandering in the wilderness, it was a real concern, especially the very severe form of ritual impurity that was caused by coming into contact with a dead body.

Let's get back to your dirty coat and how it all fits together.

Chukat (Num 19:1—22:1)

When a person in those days came into contact with a dead body and became ritually impure, the only way to remove the impurity was to take the ashes from a red heifer that had been completely burnt, mix them with some water, and then sprinkle the water on the person who had become impure. There was, however, one catch. The person whose job it was to burn the red heifer and to collect the ashes became impure. In other words, the very thing needed to make a person ritually pure, the ashes from a red heifer, made the person gathering the ashes impure.

Sounds a little like jumping into a mud puddle to get rid of the mud on your winter coat. Again, this makes no sense, but it's okay that it makes no sense. Here's why.

There are a number of different ways to think about the commandments God gives the Jewish people in the Torah. A simple one is that there are positive commandments (the kind that tell us *to* do something) and negative ones (the kind that tell us *not* to do something).

A less obvious but equally important way to think about commandments has to do with how easily they are understood. What does this mean?

There are lots of commandments that need little or no explanation, like the commandments not to murder or steal. Everyone can agree that murder and stealing are bad things, and that is why we refer to such commandments as "common-sense laws." Common-sense laws are usually things people would have decided to do or not to do even if God had not given us commandments about them.

The Torah also has a number of commandments that don't make much sense at all, and for this reason, we call them "non-common-sense laws." The best example of this involves the red heifer from this week's reading. Scholars and teachers have tried very hard over the years to explain why the same ashes from a red heifer that make some people ritually pure also make others ritually impure. They have yet to come up with a good answer.

The lack of a good answer may be a little frustrating, but people who believe in the one, true God are usually prepared to accept things that God commands even if they don't know the reason for these commandments.[2]

Think about it this way. There are times when parents ask (or maybe tell) their children to do something without giving the child an explanation. When asked why, parents sometimes respond: "Just because." And if your parents say to you, "Do this just because," you'll listen to them because you respect them and love them and trust them.

The same holds true for God. In our prayers, God is often described as our king, and we are called His servants. But just as often, He is described as a loving parent and we, His beloved children. And because of this relationship and the love and trust we have for God, we are willing to do what He asks of us, even when the request makes no sense at all.[3] This is simply what people of faith who wish to serve the one, true God do.

> *Can you think of something you might be asked to do that you would do "just because?" How about an example of something you might be asked to do that you would need to understand the reason for before doing it?*
>
> *In either case, would it make a difference who asked? Why or why not?*

---

2. This topic was also discussed at length in *A Curious Student's Guide to the Book of Exodus.*

3. While the law of the red heifer is arguably the best example of a non-common-sense law, there are other well-known examples. For instance, Jews are prohibited from wearing garments made of a combination of wool and linen (called *shatnez* in Hebrew). It's not that God's fashion sense is somehow offended by people wearing wool and linen together. This law exists just because God says so. Another excellent example is the Jewish dietary laws. Is there any good reason why Jews should only eat the meat of animals that have split hoofs and chew their cud? Is there any good reason why Jews should only eat fish that have fins and scales? No, there isn't, but it is what God has commanded.

CHUKAT (NUM 19:1—22:1)

This Makes No Sense Either!

It's not surprising that the story of the red heifer doesn't make a lot of sense. It is, after all, a not-common-sense commandment. But the next story we find in this week's reading, the one about Moses hitting a rock instead of speaking to it, doesn't seem to make much sense either.

Let's start with the details of the story.

The Jewish people have been wandering in the wilderness for forty years. During that time, according to the midrash, the Jews were accompanied by a rock that supplied them with water in Miriam's merit. (The story of this rock and how Moses first brings water from it by hitting it is found in the book of Exodus.[4]) In this week's reading, Miriam dies, and with her death, the water dries up.

Having no water to drink in the desert is not a good thing, and the people begin to panic. They surround Moses and Aaron. They scream and shout at them: "If only we had perished when our brothers perished at the instance of the LORD! Why have you brought the LORD's congregation into this wilderness for us and our beasts to die there?"

Moses and Aaron move away from the people and call out to God. God answers them, telling Moses to take his staff—the one he used to bring the plagues upon Egypt—and gather all the people together. Moses is then told to speak to the rock so that it once again brings forth water.

Seems simple enough, but there is a problem. Moses doesn't speak to the rock. He hits it. Not once but twice. Water does come pouring out of the rock, but God is not very happy with Moses (and with Aaron, who was with Moses when he hit the rock). God tells Moses that by hitting the rock instead of speaking to it, he has missed an opportunity to deepen the people's connection with

---

4. In brief, the Jews were in a place called Rephidim and had no water to drink. Moses called on God for help, and God told him to hit a certain rock with his staff. The rock split open, and water came pouring out. This rock came to be known as "Miriam's well," because, as mentioned above, the miracle was done in her merit.

God. Because of this, God tells Moses, you will not be allowed to lead the people into the land of Canaan.

What is going on here? Didn't Moses perform a miracle at God's command? Didn't he make water come pouring out of a rock? And what's more, the last time he performed this miracle, he hit the rock. What difference does it make this time if he hit the rock or spoke to it?

If you're thinking that this doesn't make sense, you're not the only one. The greatest Jewish scholars and rabbis have struggled for centuries to find answers to these questions. And while many answers have been put forward to our questions, three seem to be used most often to explain this difficult story.

The first emphasizes the power of speech. Moses is told to speak to the rock, but rocks don't have ears. Rocks can't hear. And yet, had Moses spoken to the rock, it would have heard and obeyed his words. The message here is this: if a rock, which has no ears and cannot hear, nevertheless obeys the command of God, how much more so should the Jewish people, who certainly have ears to hear God's commands, obey God. When Moses hits the rock instead of speaking to it, he misses the opportunity to teach this lesson to the Jewish people.

The second answer focuses on who is actually doing the miracle. It should be obvious, given everything the Jews in the wilderness have seen, that it is God who performs miracles like bringing water from a rock. However, when Moses replies to the shouts and screams of the people confronting him and Aaron, he says: "Shall we get water for you out of this rock?" Not "shall God get water" but "shall we get water." With this simple phrase, Moses makes it seem that it is he who will bring about this miracle, not God. This explains God's great displeasure with Moses.

The third answer is about anger. Moses has a history of sometimes getting angry. When he sees an Egyptian taskmaster beating a Hebrew slave, Moses becomes angry—so angry that he kills the Egyptian. When he meets his future wife Zipporah at the well, he sees that she and her sisters are being mistreated by the other shepherds. Moses becomes angry and chases them away. When Moses

CHUKAT (NUM 19:1—22:1)

comes down from Mount Sinai with the two stone tablets given to him by God, he sees the people dancing around the golden calf and becomes so angry that he smashes the tablets.[5]

Here, when the people complain to Moses about the lack of water, he once again becomes angry. How do we know this? He calls the people "rebels." By doing so, he is showing the people that he is angry with them, and this in turn makes the people think that God is angry with them, too. But God is *not* angry with the people. It is normal for people to be scared and worried when they are in the desert and run out of water. It is only natural to be worried under such circumstances, and God understands this. This is why He is ready to restore the well of Miriam and why He is upset with Moses for making the people think that He, God, is angry with them.

What life lessons can we learn from these very different answers?

Throughout this book, you have seen the importance of asking questions, especially when something doesn't make sense to you. This is true for life in general and for our studies of the Torah as well. What we see from this story is that it's okay to keep asking questions and to keep looking for answers. This is why there are so many answers given to try to explain what exactly Moses did wrong and why exactly God was so upset with him.

Think about it. No single answer really explains this story completely.

Hitting the rock instead of speaking to it? But Moses hit the rock the first time he brought forth water!

Suggesting that he, Moses would do the miracle? But Moses is the most humble person there ever was![6] Would anyone really believe that Moses was about to take credit for this miracle?

Losing his temper when the people were screaming and asking why he had brought them to the wilderness to die? Had he not guided them and cared for them for forty years in the wilderness?

---

5. Deut. Rabbah 3:14.

6. "Now Moses was a very humble man, more so than any other man on earth" (Num 12:3).

Who could blame Moses for being frustrated and angry when he hears the complaints of the people?

And so scholars and rabbis keep exploring the story to see if there is a better answer to be found. This is what curious people of all ages do: keep looking for good answers to their hard questions.

There is perhaps another important life lesson we can learn from this story, but it depends on which explanation of the story you think works best. If you like the third answer we gave about Moses losing his temper (and many do), we see the dangers of getting angry. When people get angry, they don't always think straight. They often say things they don't mean. And this is exactly what Moses did. Maybe he had a good reason to be angry, but his anger led him to call the people "rebels." When he did, he delivered what the people thought was a message from God, that He was angry with them. He wasn't, and Moses, in his anger, ended up delivering a false message from God. A very bad mistake for the greatest of all the biblical prophets.

> *When something happens in life that you don't understand, do you ever you ask "why" (and maybe even keep asking "why" until you get a good answer)?*
>
> *When your parents ask you to do something you don't understand or don't want to do, do you ever ask, "Why?" (and maybe even keep asking why until you get a good answer)?*
>
> *Can you see the difference between the two? Can you explain how the two are different?*

In Their Merit

As we have already seen, this week's reading tells us, with very few details, about the deaths of Miriam and Aaron. However, the midrash is there to give us more background and insights into the passing of these two righteous individuals.[7]

---

7. It is worth noting the following difference in the midrash's treatment of the deaths of Miriam and Aaron. With Miriam, the emphasis is on events

CHUKAT (NUM 19:1—22:1)

> Miriam died on the first of the month of Nisan, and the well closed up. On the first of Av, Aaron died, and the clouds of glory dissipated. On the seventh of Adar, Moses, our teacher and God's servant, died.
>
> Each had a gift that they gave to the Israelites.
>
> By the merit of Miriam, God gave the well; by the merit of Aaron, the clouds of glory; and by the merit of Moses, the Manna. When Miriam died, the well closed so the Israelites could see that it was by her merit that God granted them the well. Moses and Aaron mourned her privately, and the Israelites did so publicly.[8]

One thing that stands out in this midrash is the idea of "by the merit of." What exactly does this mean? Perhaps an example will make this clear.

Let's say your grandparents were important members of your community. They were well-known for always volunteering to help others in need. They could always be counted on to organize community programs and events. They were so liked and respected that when people meet you, they are quick to say, "Oh, you are Dolores and Harold's grandchild." They are also quick to do favors for you or help you out if you need help. In other words, you benefit directly from all the good your grandparents did, even though they did these things many years before you were even born. The benefit you get is a perfect example of "by the merit of."

What did Miriam do to build up a reserve of "merit"? Consider the following:

---

that happen after her death, such as the well drying up and the people mourning publicly for her. With Aaron, the focus is on what seems to be his fear of death. The midrash notes that when it was Aaron's time to die, Moses sought to comfort him, saying: "Your death is not like that of anyone else, for the ministering angels have come to carry you away." Moses then adds: "Is my death then going to be like your death? For when you die, you will have me to bury you, but when I die, I will not have my brother to bury me. When you die, your sons inherit your position as high priest, but when I die, others will inherit my honor." He thus comforted Aaron with his words.

8. Otzar Midrashim, Beit Hamidrash, Hadar Alef.

The talmudic rabbis list Miriam as one of seven Jewish prophetesses.[9] From a young age, this gift gave her great courage and strength. For instance, when she was only six years old, she challenged her father, Amram, who, as leader of the Jews in Egypt, encouraged families to stop having babies. Amram knew that the Egyptians would kill any baby boy born to a Jewish mother. Miriam reminded him that if the Jews didn't have babies, no girls would be born either. Hearing this, Amram told families to start having babies again.

Miriam was equally brave when she watched over her baby brother Moses after their mother, Jochebed, placed him in the Nile River in a wicker basket. It was Miriam who then stood before Pharaoh's daughter and suggested that she find a Hebrew woman to nurse the baby.

As an adult, during the forty years the Jewish people were wandering in the wilderness, Miriam worked with her two brothers to guide and support the people: Moses taught Torah, Aaron served as the high priest, and Miriam taught the women.[10]

Miriam was a role model and an inspiration to the women of her generation. Here is just one example. We read in the book of Exodus that Miriam led the women in songs of praise at the splitting of the Sea of Reeds.[11] As they sang, the women took tambourines in their hands. The midrash famously asks, "How did the women of this generation know to take tambourines out of Egypt, when there was barely enough time to take food?" The answer, of course, is Miriam. She had taught the women to have faith in God, and their faith was so strong that they were certain God would perform miracles for them in the desert. So, they brought tambourines out of Egypt to have when they would sing songs of praise and thanks to God.

---

9. The seven are Sarah, Miriam, Deborah, Hannah, Abigail, Huldah, and Esther, and the Talmud (Megillah 14a) brings proof texts to demonstrate the prophetic status of each of them.

10. Targum Micha 6:4.

11. The Hebrew name of the sea, *Yam Suf*, is often incorrectly translated as "the Red Sea." The correct translation is "the Sea of Reeds."

Chukat (Num 19:1—22:1)

And what of Aaron? What was the source of his great "merit?"

We all know that Aaron was at Moses's side whenever he confronted Pharaoh. We know that it was Aaron who performed each of the first three plagues.[12] And, of course, Aaron was selected by God Himself to be the first high priest to serve in the mishkan. Yet, in the Jewish tradition, Aaron is perhaps best known as a man who "loved peace, pursued peace, loved people and brought them closer to Torah."[13]

How great was Aaron's love of peace? According to the midrash, if Aaron ever saw two people fighting, he would go to one of them and say, "I just saw your friend. He is very sad about your fight. He thinks it's all his fault, and now he is wondering how he can ever face you again." Aaron would then go to the second person and say the exact same thing. And what do you think happened the next time these two individuals saw each other? They would apologize to each other and make up.

Aaron was also credited with saving many marriages, because when a husband and wife would get into a big fight, he would use the same strategy to get them back together. Aaron was so successful in doing this that the midrash tells us that thousands of children were named after him (because they would not have been born had Aaron not been there to save the parents' marriages).

The concept of "by the merit of" is very important in Judaism, and Miriam and Aaron are just two examples of it. But they are excellent role models to keep in mind as you try to do things in your own life that will help you build your own reserve of "merit" that someday in turn will help your children and grandchildren.

> *List three things your parents do that help you out "in their merit." What have these things taught you? How can you try to imitate them?*

---

12. The text in Exodus tells us that Aaron takes Moses's staff and performs the first three plagues: turning the waters of the Nile River into blood, bringing swarms of frogs from the river, and turning the dust of Egypt into lice. This is because Moses was indebted to the Nile for saving him as a baby and to the dust for saving him as an adult (after he hid the body of the Egyptian taskmaster there).

13. Pirkei Avot 1:12.

Balak

(Num 22:2—25:9)

Part One (For Parents and Educators): Who is the Greater Prophet, Moses or Balaam?

Several of the weekly readings in the book of Numbers, like Korach and Pinchas, are named for the reading's main character. Others, like Naso (the census) and Shelach (sending out the spies), make reference to the main event in the reading in the title of the reading itself. This week's reading, Balak, does neither. Its main character is Balaam, who is the subject of much debate and discussion, both in the Talmud and in the midrash.

Who is Balaam, and what type of person is he?

It is clear from our reading this week that Balaam has a big ego and believes that there is little he cannot do. This is due in part to the way he is treated by the people of his generation. For example, when the king of Midian sends messengers to Balaam seeking his help fighting the Jews, the king instructs the messengers to say to Balaam: "I know that he whom you bless is blessed indeed, and he whom you curse is cursed."

We also see that he is very greedy and is prepared to do almost anything for money. How do we know this? God specifically tells Balaam (as we will see) not to go with these messengers. According to the midrash, instead of telling the messengers the truth, Balaam hints that they have not offered him enough money to go with them. It is as if he were saying to the messengers: "Your king ought to give me all his silver and gold because without me, he would have to hire many armies to fight against Jews."[1]

Despite all this, the rabbis of the Talmud state that Balaam is one of the ancient world's seven non-Jewish prophets,[2] and he is seen by these rabbis as the greatest of the seven—so great that the midrash says that he was as respected and listened to in the non-Jewish world as Moses was among the Jews.[3]

What is so very interesting is that the earliest of these sources see Balaam merely as someone who could interpret dreams. In later sources, his abilities grow to the point where he becomes something like a sorcerer, until finally, he receives the spirit of prophecy. But Balaam's gift of prophecy is unlike that of any other prophet, for he is said to have the ability to know the exact moment when God is angry.[4] (In this week's reading, Balaam intends to use this gift to trick God and thus be allowed to curse the Jewish people.)

The verse in Deuteronomy declares that "never again did there arise in Israel a prophet like Moses," but according to the midrash, "One has arisen among the nations!"[5] This, of course, is Balaam.

These sources go on to present Balaam as in no way inferior to Moses, either in wisdom or in the gift of prophecy. Moses may have been the greatest prophet among the Jews, but Balaam was his equal among the non-Jews of those days. Comparing the two, it could be argued that Moses was greater because God called him without any previous preparation on Moses's part. For Balaam to receive the word of God, he had to offer sacrifices (which he does seven times in this week's reading). But Balaam had one advantage over Moses. Moses had to pray to God "to show him His ways."

---

1. The midrash further says that Balaam's ego is also seen in his answer because he suggests that even with these additional armies, it is not certain that Midian could defeat the Jews. Balaam claims that with his help, Midian's victory would be a sure thing.

2. The other six were Beor (Balaam's father), Job, and Job's four friends (see B. Bava Batra 15b).

3. Numbers Rabbah 14:20.

4. B. Berakhot 7a.

5. *Sifrei Deuteronomy* 357.

Balak (Num 22:2—25:9)

Balaam, as he describes himself in this week's reading, was the man who "knew the knowledge of the Most High."

At this point, you might be wondering, what's going on here? How does a person shown in this week's reading to be greedy and an egotist end up been described in the Talmud and the midrash as a great man, one equal to Moses himself?

The answer is that the rabbis of the Talmud understood a very simple truth. Part of the greatness of the Jewish people comes from the fact that they had Moses as a teacher and a leader. This is why these rabbis believe that God gave Balaam to the non-Jewish world of that time. By doing so, God makes sure these non-Jewish nations cannot claim that if they had had a prophet like Moses, they too could have received the Torah.

In the end, was Balaam actually as great as Moses? Of course not. When Balaam refuses to listen to God and instead goes to try and curse the Jewish people, God sends an angel to kill him. The great Balaam cannot even see this angel, but the donkey he is riding does. Compare this to Moses, who goes up Mount Sinai to speak to God "face-to-face."

The tragedy of Balaam is that he misses the opportunity for true and lasting greatness. Balaam, who imagines himself gaining great wealth and even greater fame for cursing the Jewish people, is forced to admit his powerlessness in the face of God's opposition: "I could not of my own accord do anything good or bad contrary to the LORD's command. What the LORD says, that I must say."

Balak

(Num 22:2—25:9)

Part Two: Turning Curses into Blessings

Summary of This Week's Reading

As we begin this week's reading, we find the Jewish people at the border of Moab. Before arriving there, the Jewish army conquers the two neighbors of Moab, the Amorites and the Bashanites. This makes Balak, king of Moab, fearful that his nation will be the next military target. He therefore forms an alliance (which is like a partnership) with the rulers of another neighboring country, Midian, and begins to plan how he might defeat the Jews. This plan centers on Balaam, a great non-Jewish prophet and sorcerer. Balak sends messengers to Balaam to ask him to come and curse the Jews.

    Balaam listens to the messengers but tells them that he must first speak with God before answering them. God appears to Balaam that night and tells him not to go to Moab. "You shall not curse the people because they are blessed!"

    Balaam sends word with Balak's messengers that God will not allow him to do as the king asks. Balak, who won't take no for an answer, sends another group of messengers to Balaam and promises him great riches in return for his services. Once again, God appears to Balaam. This time, God allows Balaam to go—provided he only speak the words that God dictates to him. But God is disappointed with Balaam's attitude and his continued desire to curse the Jews. God therefore sends an angel with a drawn sword to block Balaam's

Balak (Num 22:2—25:9)

path. Ironically, the great prophet Balaam cannot see the angel, but the donkey he is riding does. She refuses to move forward on the road they are traveling. Balaam becomes so angry with his donkey that he beats her three different times. (He of course does not realize that the donkey saved his life by refusing to move.)

At this point, the donkey miraculously speaks and scolds Balaam for beating her. God then "opens Balaam's eyes," and he sees the angel. The angel also scolds Balaam for his behavior toward his donkey and reminds him that he may only say what God dictates to him.

After this humbling episode, Balaam arrives in Moab, where he is greeted by King Balak. Balaam tells Balak to build seven altars and to offer sacrifices to God. God then speaks to Balaam and tells him exactly what to say. No curses. Only blessings. Balaam is forced to say: "How can I damn (or curse) whom God has not damned, how doom when the LORD has not doomed?" Balaam goes on to glorify the Jewish people with beautiful blessings and praises. When Balak responds angrily to the blessings, Balaam reminds him that he can only say that which God tells him to say.

Neither Balak nor Balaam wants to concede defeat or abandon their mission. Balak takes Balaam to another location, hoping that a change of place will permit a different outcome. They again build altars and offer sacrifices, and again God tells Balaam to bless the Jewish people. Balaam says, "When He blesses, I cannot reverse it . . . The LORD their God is with them."

This pattern—moving to a new place, building more altars, and trying to curse the Jews but in the end blessing them—happens five more times (making for a total of seven failed attempts at cursing the Jews). In the end, Balaam is forced to utter an undeniable truth: "Those who bless [them] shall be blessed, and those who curse [them] shall be cursed." Balak, angry and frustrated, sends Balaam away.

But Balaam isn't done with the Jews, at least according to the midrash. He suggests to the leaders of Moab and Midian that they send their women to seduce the Jewish men. Sadly, many of the Jewish men cannot resist, and they hug and kiss these women. They are even tricked into worshipping their god, who is called Baal Peor.

>God is very angry to see this, and He commands Moses to execute the guilty people. At the same time, God unleashes a deadly plague upon the Jewish people. Many die, and many more would have died but for the actions of Aaron's grandson Phinehas.
>
>The story pauses here but continues in next week's reading, and that is where we will discuss in detail what Phinehas does to stop the plague and save the people.

Life Lessons from Balak

A major theme of this week's reading is opposites, or perhaps more correctly, of things changing and becoming their opposites. The best example is the curses Balaam intends to speak against the Jewish people but which, in the end, God turns into blessings. But there are some life lessons here about things that don't change and should not change. Let's see what they are.

Not Just for Adults

The stories in this week's reading can seem a little confusing: a prophet who thinks he can ignore God's command; a talking donkey; curses that end up as blessings. These certainly will cause us to ask some hard questions. They will also lead us to talk about topics that people think are only for adults but that actually aren't. They involve lessons that apply to people of all ages.

Here's one to get us started: self-awareness.

If this sounds complicated, it can be, but it doesn't have to be. Self-awareness means knowing yourself very well. It means understanding things you do well and like to do. It also means recognizing things you do less well and, when necessary, working to get better at these things.

Think about this example. At some point, every student is asked to answer a question in class or perhaps make a presentation to the whole class. Maybe you don't like doing this. Maybe it makes you nervous or even a little scared. But to do well in school,

BALAK (NUM 22:2—25:9)

to become a better student, you will need to learn how to be less nervous and less scared.

Admitting that the reason you don't answer questions in class isn't that you don't want to but because it makes you nervous is a sign that you are self-aware. Balaam is *not* self-aware, and this is one of the reasons his story turns out so badly in the end.

Of course, Balaam is aware that he has been given the gift of prophecy. We see this in his response to the messengers sent to him by Balak, king of Moab: "Spend the night here, and I shall reply to you as the LORD may instruct me." Look carefully at his answer. Balaam has no doubt that God will answer him (although, as we will see, Balaam does not get the answer he wants or expects).

This is where Balaam's self-awareness ends. Yes, he knows God will answer him when he calls out to Him. But he incorrectly thinks that God will always listen to him and always let him do whatever he wants to do. Balaam even thinks he can trick God into changing His mind if God turns down his request.

How could Balaam be so mistaken? How could he be so lacking in self-awareness?

The answer is simple. Balaam has a big ego. He is the greatest gentile prophet of his time, as great as Moses in some ways. But he lacks Moses's humility. This is why he believes those who praise him and tell him how great he is. This is why he lets those compliments go to his head and feed his ego. By doing do, Balaam loses sight of the things he cannot do, and ignoring what you cannot do does show a lack of self-awareness. By ignoring his limitations and challenging God, Balaam angers God,, and God shows Balaam the error of his ways in a very humiliating way.

Picture the scene. Messengers from Moab have come to Balaam asking him to curse the Jewish people. (The king of Moab thinks that if Balaam curses the Jews, he, the king, can defeat them in battle.) God tells Balaam not to go, but Balaam insists on going. God tells Balaam that he may not curse the Jews, but Balaam thinks he can fool God and somehow, in the end, curse the Jews. Talk about lacking self-awareness! Balaam certainly should have known that a human cannot fool God.

By this time, God has had enough of Balaam. He sends an angel with a fiery sword in its hand to strike Balaam. Three times the angel appears before Balaam. Balaam doesn't see the angel, but his donkey does. And so, three times, the donkey turns from the road she's on to save Balaam. Balaam, who does not see the angel, gets angrier and angrier at the donkey. Three times Balaam beats the donkey with a stick, until the donkey says: "What have I done to you that you have beaten me these three times?" Balaam is not surprised or shocked by a talking donkey. He is just angry at her and tells her he would have killed her if had a sword. It is at this point that God allows Balaam to see the angel. The angel mocks Balaam, asking: "Why did you beat your donkey?" The angel then scolds Balaam, saying: "If she had not shied away from me, you are the one I should have killed, while sparing her."

A true prophet, a self-aware prophet, would have recognized a talking donkey for the miracle it is. A true prophet would have seen the angel himself and not needed a donkey to warn him about the angel. This is what Balaam's ego and lack of self-awareness brings about. Balaam, who is so convinced he can fool God, sees the talking donkey as an inconvenience instead of a miracle.

Balaam's lack of self-awareness angers God and puts Balaam in a situation in which he should feel embarrassed and humiliated. After all, God allows a donkey to see a vision of an angel but denies this vision to this supposedly great prophet. What's the moral to this story? A talking donkey is something you will never see, but a person being embarrassed by doing something silly or inappropriate because he or she is lacking in self-awareness? Sadly, that is something we see too often in life.

> *Let's see how self-aware you are. List three things you do well and why you enjoy doing them. Next, list three things you do less well and what you are doing to do to improve in these areas. Finally, share your lists with your parents and ask if they agree with your lists.*

BALAK (NUM 22:2—25:9)

What's Mine is Mine

No one thinks being greedy is a good thing, and this is particularly true in Judaism. The Jewish sages of the Talmud think of greed as a character flaw and describe it in an interesting way.

> There are four types of character in human beings: One that says: "mine is mine, and yours is yours": this is a commonplace type. [One that says:] "mine is yours and yours is mine": is an unlearned person (*am aaretz*); [One that says:] "mine is yours and yours is yours" is a pious person. [One that says:] "mine is mine, and yours is mine" is a wicked person.[1]

It is normal, says the Talmud, not to want to share ("mine is mine, and yours is yours"), and there is nothing wrong with being normal. Regularly sharing without expecting anything in return ("mine is yours and yours is yours") is described as "pious," which, in the times of the Talmud, was the highest compliment you could give. In other words, sharing was thought of as something very special. But greed? Not sharing at all—and worse than that, wanting the other person's portion, too ("mine is mine, and yours is mine")? There is only one word for it: wicked.

Of these four character traits, it is the last that best describes Balaam. This can be understood from the story itself, even if it is not stated explicitly. Balaam is motivated by greed. He is already honored and respected as a great prophet. Doing the bidding of the king of Midian would not bring him more honor or more respect. What could possibly be in it for Balaam? A big payoff, that is, lots of money.

---

1. Pirkei Avot 5:10.

We see a hint of this in the text itself, when Balaam says to the messengers: "Though Balak were to give me his house full of silver and gold, I could not do anything, big or little, contrary to the command of the LORD my God." It is as if Balaam were saying to the messengers: "I won't do it for what you've offered to pay me, but if the king pays me more—a lot more—than I'm his man."

Balaam's greed causes him to ignore God. Balaam wants to curse the Jewish people and make himself rich by doing so. God says no, but Balaam tries anyway. He tries a total of seven times, and each time, God forces him to bless the Jewish people, not curse them.[2] Each time this happens, the king of Moab gets madder and madder. He finally chases Balaam away and tells him to return to his home. However, Balaam never reaches his home. When war ultimately breaks out between the Jews and Moab, Balaam is caught up in the battle. According to the midrash, Jewish soldiers execute him, saying: "You attacked us with our [weapon, that is, the power of speech]; we are attacking you with yours [the sword]."[3]

To close our discussion of the dangers of greed, let's take a look at one more story. This is not a Jewish story. It actually comes to us from the ancient Greeks, and it is the source of the expression "having a golden touch." It involves a rich and greedy king named Midas.

In this story, Midas is a rich king who has everything a king could wish for. He lives in a great castle, which makes him very happy. He has a beautiful daughter, whom he loves very much. (Interestingly, the story tells us nothing of his wife.) Despite all this, what makes Midas happiest is gold. He is so attached to his gold that he spends his days simply counting his golden coins. Sometimes he even covers his body with gold objects, as if he wanted to bathe in them. In short, Midas is obsessed with gold.

One day, Dionysus, the Greek god of wine, passes through the kingdom of Midas. One of Dionysus's friends who is travelling

---

2. As a lasting irony, Jews to this day have a custom of saying one of Balaam's curses turned blessing every time they enter a synagogue. The verse, found in Num 24:5, reads: "How fair are your tents, O Jacob, Your dwellings, O Israel!"

3. Midrash HaGadol, Bamidbar 31:8.

with him becomes tired. He decides to take a nap in the famous rose gardens surrounding the palace of king Midas, where the king finds him, asleep. The king recognizes him as a friend of Dionysus and invites him to spend a few days at his palace. When Dionysus hears how Midas took care of his friend, he promises Midas to grant any wish he desires. Midas thinks for a long time and then says: "I wish for everything I touch to become gold." Dionysus warns the king to think carefully about his wish, but Midas knows (or thinks he knows) what he wants.

Starting the next day, everything Midas touches turns to gold, just as he wished for. He runs through his palace all morning long touching everything in sight: tables, chairs, carpets, doors, even his bathtub. This goes on until Midas grows tired and hungry. He decides it is time for breakfast. Without even thinking, he reaches for a grape to eat, but it turns into gold! The same happens with a slice of bread and a glass of water. Suddenly, Midas is scared. Tears fills his eyes, and at that very moment, his beloved daughter enters the room. Once again, Midas does not think before he acts. He hugs his daughter, and she turns into a golden statue. What started as his greatest wish turns out to be his worst nightmare.

Unlike the story of Balaam, Midas's story has a happy ending. Horrified by what happened to his daughter, he prays to Dionysus, who hears his prayer and feels sorry for him. Dionysus tells Midas to go to Pactolus River and wash his hands. Midas does so, and when he thrusts his hands into the river, he is amazed to see gold flowing from his hands. When he returns home, everything he touched, including his daughter, has become normal again.

Midas is lucky. In the end, everything works out for him. But typically, stories of greed do not end well for the people involved, and that is one of the important life lessons we learn from Balaam.

Do you or your family know any stories, be they true and made up, about greed? How do things turn out in your stories? Any happy endings?

I'll Do That (Not)

We saw how Balaam tried and failed seven different times to curse the Jews, even though he had told the king of Moab he would do exactly that. We learned an important lesson about the dangers of being greedy from that story. But there is another life lesson to be found here, and it involves overpromising.

Overpromising is just what it sounds like: promising to do more than you're able to do. In many cases, we know why a person will overpromise. It could be because of ego. Or because they're embarrassed to say no. Or maybe to impress their friends. Or maybe, as in the case of Balaam, it's a matter of greed.

In the end, the reason isn't so important. What matters is that a person promises to do something and cannot do it. And more often than not, this leads to bad outcomes. Feelings get hurt. People get frustrated. And sometimes, as in the story of Balaam, really bad things can happen.

This may be why we see Balaam keep trying and trying and trying. Balaam promised Balak that he could and would curse the Jewish people. God, however, would not allow this to happen. This being the case, a single example of Balaam's curses being turned into blessing would have shown us that he had overpromised. But Balaam seems unable or unwilling to admit that he overpromised, He tries again and again and again, seven times in total, to curse the Jews.

With this story, the Torah highlights for us how easy it is to get trapped by over promising, and how bad the consequences of over promising can be. It took Balaam seven tries and seven failures to learn this lesson. And, in truth, the outcome was very bad for him. By spending so much time on this story, the Torah is trying to help us avoid repeating Balaam's mistakes as well as the bad things that always seem to result from over promising.

> *What do you think a person should do if they realize that they have overpromised? Should they do it anyway just to be able to say that they tried? Should they just admit they can't do it? In either case, is someone owed an explanation? An apology?*

Pinchas

(Num 25:10—30:1)

Summary of This Week's Reading

Last week's reading concluded with Moabite and Midianite women tricking many Jewish men into idol worship. God sends a plague to punish the sinners, and the plague only stops when Phinehas kills a leader of the sinners, a man who openly mocked both God and Moses.

This week's reading begins with God praising Phinehas for his actions and rewarding his bravery by making him and his descendants priests. God then commands the Jews to punish the Midianites by going out to war against them. (We will read about this war in next week's reading.)

With a war looming and the people soon to enter the land of Canaan, God commands Moses and Elazar the high priest to take a census of all males over the age of twenty. (If you remember from the opening of the book of Numbers, a census involves counting people.) Our reading gives us the total number of people in each tribe as well as a combined total (601,730). The tribe of Levi is not included in this census, because they are priests and not soldiers and because their tribe will not inherit a portion in the land.[1]

   1. Everyone knows that Jacob had twelve sons and that each son was the founder of a tribe of Israel. However, the list of tribes changes depending on why the tribes are being listed. The list of sons includes both Levi and Joseph. The list of tribes for purpose of dividing the land is different. Joseph received a special blessing from Jacob (called the birthright), which meant that he was entitled to two portions in the land. And so, his two grandsons, Ephraim and

Once the census is complete, God explains how the numbers are to be used. The land of Canaan is to be divided among all those who are counted in this census, with the location of each tribe's portion determined by lottery. (We will discuss exactly how this is to be done shortly.)

Two important things happen after Moses receives God's command about how to divide up the land. First, the tribe of Levi is counted. (There are 23,000 Levite males above the age of one month.) Second, the five daughters of a man named Zelophehad come to Moses with a big problem. The plan he shared with the people for dividing the land only includes sons, but their father, who died in the desert, only had daughters. Should they not get any land simply because they are women?

Moses sees that this is a very good question, and he is not quite sure how to answer it. He turns to God for help, and God tells him that these five women are correct that they should inherit their father's portion in the land of Canaan. (We will have more to say about this story later.)

We next read how God tells Moses to climb to the top of Mount Abarim. While Moses is not allowed to enter the land of Canaan, he can at least see the Promised Land before he dies. Moses asks God to appoint a worthy individual to lead the people after he dies. God agrees and tells Moses to publicly announce to the people that Joshua will take over as leader once he, Moses, dies.

From this point until the end of our reading, we read all the details of the various communal sacrifices that were offered in the mishkan. This includes the twice-daily Tamid sacrifice as well as the additional sacrifices offered on the Sabbath and Rosh Chodesh (the first day of the Jewish month). We also read about the sacrifices offered on all the major Jewish holidays: Passover, Shavuot, Rosh Hashanah, Yom Kippur, Sukkot, and Shemini Atzeret.

Manasseh, each receive a portion. To keep the number of tribes at twelve, Levi does not get a portion of land. His tribe's "portion" is the priesthood and the privilege of serving in the mishkan.

PINCHAS (NUM 25:10—30:1)

Life Lessons from Pinchas

This may be a short reading, but it contains several life lessons that are as important today as they were when these stories took place. As we do each week, we will focus on three in particular.

Hero or Zealot?

The story of Phinehas, which we began in last week's reading and which continues in our reading this week, is complicated and perhaps a bit confusing. It is not clear even to the most curious of students what life lessons it has to offer us. But it is an important story in this history of the Jewish people's wanderings through the Sinai wilderness, one we dare not skip or ignore.

You may recall that God forces Balaam to bless the Jewish people rather than curse them. But Balaam still wants to harm the Jews, so he convinces the leaders of Moab to use their daughters to trick the Jewish men into sinning. Sadly, his plan works. A large number of Jewish men do act inappropriately with these women, and they even end up worshipping the gods of the Moabites!

This makes God very angry. He once again sends a plague to strike the sinners and commands Moses to execute their leaders. But before Moses can act, one of the tribal leaders, a man named Zimri, brings a Moabite princess, Cozbi, before Moses. Zimri mocks Moses for trying to keep the Jewish men away from the Moabite women. To prove his point, Zimri acts inappropriately with Cozbi right in front of Moses. Moses is so shocked by Zimri's actions that he can neither speak nor act. Phinehas sees all this and understands that Zimri is not only mocking Moses but God as well. He decides to defend the honor of Moses and of God Himself by killing Zimri and Cozbi. As soon as he does, the plague stops.

There is an important principle in Jewish law that a person may violate or ignore any of God's commandments to save another person's life. Did Phinehas know that the plague would stop if he killed Zimri? No, but even if he did, could he really murder Zimri to save the lives of the people dying in the plague?

The answer is not so simple.

To understand the story and the character of Phinehas, we first have to understand what a zealot is. A zealot is a fanatic or an extremist. He or she is a person who will not compromise his or her beliefs. For zealots, there is nothing more important than their religious or political ideals. But the truth is, defining who is a zealot, and figuring out whether that is a good or bad thing, is much harder and much more complicated.

There is little doubt that Phinehas was a zealot. For us, then, the real question to answer is, were Phinehas's actions proper and praiseworthy, or did he cross the line and simply commit murder?

The talmudic sages recognize the daring of Phinehas's actions. Some sages even think that killing Zimri was legal.[2] Others disagree. They say that the leaders of that generation wished to expel Phinehas from the community for his act. In fact, according to this view, had Zimri turned on Phinehas and killed him, he would have deserved no punishment at all.

This uncertainty about how to interpret Phinehas's act is not limited to the talmudic sages. Later scholars conclude that acts of zealotry (like those of Phinehas) should not be encouraged. This is because a zealot, from a Jewish perspective, needs to be motivated by an unselfish desire to defend the glory of God. In the end, who can tell what really is in the zealot's heart and mind? Is he defending God, or is he committing murder? It was this uncertainty that led some to argue that Phinehas should have been thrown out of the community.

There is another point to consider. Zimri may have deserved to be killed because of the seriousness of his sin. But Phinehas killed him without a trial. By doing so, Phinehas took the law into his own hands, which is never a good thing.

So, Phinehas's actions were inappropriate and possibly illegal. Or were they?

There are a number of rabbis and Jewish scholars who disagree with this point of view. They ask, Why was it important for us to know Zimri's name? Was his name really such an important

---

2. B. Sanhedrin 82a.

Pinchas (Num 25:10—30:1)

part of the story? Yes, it was, because by mentioning his name, the story is telling us that Phinehas did not hesitate to kill Zimri even though he was a tribal prince and there was a risk that his fellow tribesmen would seek revenge for his death. This means that Phinehas should be praised for putting himself in danger in order to do the "right thing." Phinehas endangers himself for the sake of the Jewish people, proving that he has no other interest than avenging the dishonor shown God by Zimri and the others.

So, Phinehas's actions were a good thing. Or were they?

There were consequences to Phinehas' actions. Some believe that prior to killing Zimri, Moses thought Phinehas would replace him as leader. However, once Moses saw the zealotry of Phinehas, he understood that Phinehas lacked the character traits necessary to be a successful leader, even though Moses thought of Phinehas as holier than others. Moses understood better than anyone else that a leader must conduct himself with moderation and flexibility.

So, what are we to make of Phineas's actions?

Phinehas acts in an extreme manner and, we have to admit, in a zealous manner. But he acts in the face of an ongoing plague in which twenty-four thousand people have already died. Bottom line, these were extraordinary circumstances, and as such, they demanded extraordinary action.

Phinehas teaches us that sometimes we must act before we think, perhaps even in a zealous manner. His story also teaches us that there will inevitably be consequences to our actions when they are driven by zealotry. Sometimes, we just cannot be sure of what those consequences will be.

There is an important postscript to this story. (A postscript is something that comes at the end of a story that tells us a little more about the story.) It is as confusing as the story itself.

God Himself says that Phinehas acts as a zealot.[3] But God also says that He is not destroying the Jewish people due to the

---

3. Numbers 25:10–11. There is no consensus among the many translations of this verse regarding the Hebrew word *bekan'o*. All agree that this word describes the reason why Phinehas acts, but some translate it as "zealous" and others as "jealous."

actions of Phinehas. God seems to understand the seriousness of Phinehas's action and the risks he faces. This is why God extends His protection to Phinehas in the form of His "covenant of peace." But God also rewards Phinehas by making him a priest and thus permitting him to serve in the mishkan.[4]

> Ask your parents about someone they thought of as a zealot when they were younger.[5] Why did they think that person was a zealot? Do they still think of the person as a zealot? Why or why not? What has changed to change their opinion of that person?

That's Not Fair

How many times have you heard one of your friends say, "That's not fair!"? Probably a lot, and this ought to make you stop and think, What is fair? Are some things always fair, or is it a matter of who's asking and when? These are good questions, and this week's reading has some interesting insights on what's fair and what's not.

---

4. When God selects Aaron to be high priest, God adds that Aaron's sons and their sons after them will also serve as priests in the mishkan. Phinehas, while he was a grandson of Aaron, had already been born by this time, so this promise did not apply to him. Only now, as a reward for his act of zealotry, does Phinehas become a priest.

5. There are many examples in American history of individuals who were thought of as zealots in their lifetimes but whom, as the generations pass, have come to be seen as heroic and patriotic. These include virtually all of America's "founding fathers" as well as Harriet Tubman, Abraham Lincoln, Susan B. Anthony, and Martin Luther King, Jr. (or anyone in the Civil Rights movement). There are certainly politicians today, both on the right and the left, who are thought of as zealots. Whether they will still be seen by future generations as zealots is as open question.

PINCHAS (NUM 25:10—30:1)

As we have noted before, the book of Numbers takes place in the fortieth year of the Jews' wanderings in the Sinai wilderness. Here, in this week's reading, they continue their preparations to enter the land of Canaan. They have been counted (yet again), and God now tells Moses how to divide the land among the twelve tribes.

From God's instructions, it is clear that He is interested in a fair division of the land. He tells Moses that the land is to be divided so that every family gets what we sometimes call a "family plot." This is why the verse tells us that the land is to be divided "according to the listed names" gathered in the most recent census. Each tribe is also to get a portion. This, too, seems fair and makes sense.

There is just one catch. God's instructions to Moses end with "With larger groups increase the share, with smaller groups reduce the share. Each is to be assigned its share according to its enrollment [that is, its count in the census]." What exactly does God mean by "larger groups" and "smaller groups?"

One view is that God is referring to the tribes, meaning that the tribes with more people are to get larger portions in the land of Canaan. For example, the tribe of Judah, whose count in this week's census is 76,500 should receive much more land than the tribe of Gad, which only numbers 40,500. As for individual families, every family would get the same size piece of land.

Seems only fair, right?

However, there is a second view about how to divide the land. According to those who follow this view, the most important thing

God says in His instructions on how to divide the land is "according to the listed names." This means that larger families (say, with six or eight children) would get more land than smaller families (which might only have two or three children). To achieve this, each tribe would get the same amount of land.

This, too, seems reasonable.

The point is, we have here two very different suggestions on how to divide the land, and *both* seem fair. Both make sense. On a practical level, Moses has to pick one or the other, and most rabbis and scholars believe that he used the first approach, that is, the tribes with more people got more land, as you can see in the map below.

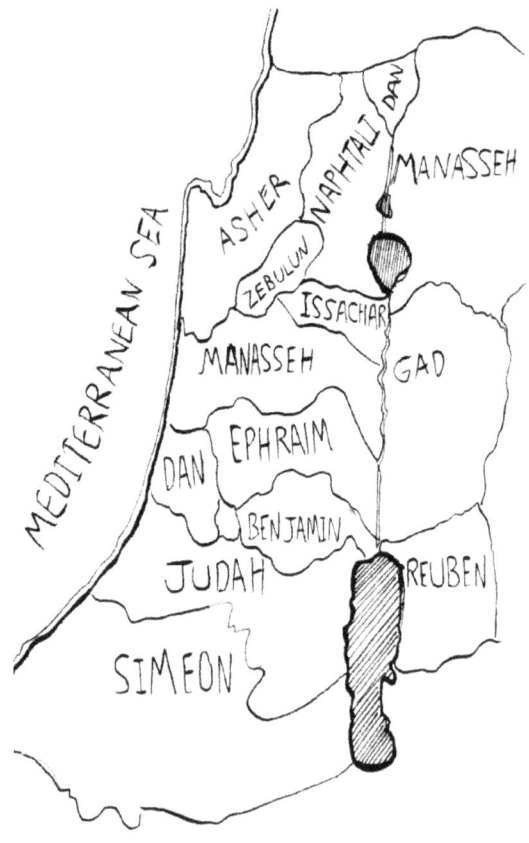

Pinchas (Num 25:10—30:1)

At first glance this all seems like a simple math problem. What is the best way to divide up the land? But what we see is that questions of fairness can depend on who is asking. In this case, if we were to ask the leaders of the tribes which they thought was the fairest way to split up the land, what do you think they'd say? Tribes with more people need and deserve more land, of course. But if we then turned to individual families and asked the same question, they would probably say that bigger families need more land.

This is a really good lesson to keep in mind the next time you or one of your friends complains that something is unfair. How one defines what is fair depends on who is asking the question. In other words, something that seems quite unfair to one person might be very fair to someone else.

> What do you do when you and a friend can't agree on what's fair? Do you do it your friend's way? Your way? Or do you figure out something that lets you both get some (but not all) of what you wanted? In the end, do you think that this compromise is actually the most fair?

Women Have Rights, Too

In the middle of this week's reading, we find a very short and very interesting story. This story, which is all of seven verses long, is about the five daughters of a man called Zelophehad. At the heart of their story is a complaint about their status as women.

In those days, when a man died, his sons inherited all of his property. Even though Zelophehad died in the Sinai wilderness before reaching Canaan, his heirs (that is, his children who inherit his property) have a claim to a portion of land in Canaan. Since Zelophehad had only daughters, it seemed that his land would go unclaimed or be taken over by someone in his tribe of Manasseh. If this were to happen, the family name of Zelophehad would disappear, and his daughters do not think this is right or fair.

These women bring their complaint to Moses, who understands that they are asking an important and a valid question.

Why can't they inherit their father's property? A good question for which Moses has no answer. He turns to God for advice, and God agrees with the daughters, telling Moses: "The plea of Zelophehad daughters is just: you should give them a hereditary holding among their father's kinsmen; transfer their father's share to them."

There is much we can learn from the story of these five women.

Let's start with a very basic question. How could Moses not know the law in this case? Surely the man who spent forty days and nights on Mount Sinai learning the law from God Himself would know how to resolve this issue. Yet Moses is at a loss as to what to do. What's going on?

Believe it or not, the fact that Moses does not know what to say to these women has nothing to do with him. The law about daughters inheriting their father's property when he has no sons should have been written by Moses, as was the case with most laws in the Torah. In other words, these laws should have been taught to the people by Moses without any need for some unique event to make the law public. Why, then, is this law so different that it is not included with all the other laws previously taught to Moses? Quite simply, it is a reflection of the greatness of the daughters of Zelophehad.[6] Their merit and standing was so high that God determined that these laws should be, as it were, written through them because the law was taught to everyone because of their question.

A second lesson speaks to the character of these women themselves. Their story is about devotion to family, to nation, and to homeland. More important, theirs is a story about strong women, brave women, who help shape the future of the Jewish people as they stand ready to enter the land of Canaan. There are few stories like it in the Torah, and young girls truly benefit from reading about such strong role models.

---

6. What is the source of their great merit? The biblical commentators point out that the verses in this week's reading trace the daughters' family tree back to Joseph. They note that the Promised Land of Israel was very special to Joseph, as it says in the book of Genesis: "So Joseph made the sons of Israel swear, saying, 'When God has taken notice of you, you shall carry up my bones from here.'" So, too, did the daughters of Zelophehad hold the land dear, as is made clear from the verse in our reading: "Give us an inheritance."

PINCHAS (NUM 25:10—30:1)

But make no mistake. These women are role models for young boys, too. They are quick to stand up for what they believe to be right, even if it means challenging a leader as great as Moses.

Sometimes it can be hard to stand up for what we believe, whether we're adults or children. It can sometimes be awkward or uncomfortable to do so. It can upset others or make things difficult for us when we do so. These daughters knew what they faced. Women in those days did not always stand up for themselves or make their complaints public, especially to the leaders of their community. But the daughters of Zelophehad did, and their actions should inspire all of us to do so whenever we can.

> *Can you think of a time when you wanted to stand up for yourself but didn't? Why didn't you? Now that you've read about the daughters of Zelophehad, do you think you will stand up for yourself the next time? Why?*

Matot

(Num 30:2—32:42)

Summary of This Week's Reading

There is no other way to put it: this week's reading isn't very child-friendly. It recounts a bloody, brutal war waged by the Jews at the command of God against the armies of Midian. Why? Because Midian partnered with Moab in the plan to trick the Jewish men into sinning.

The victory of the Jewish army, led by Phinehas, is swift and complete. There are no enemy survivors. (This is the battle in which Balaam is killed.) But the Jews do return with the women and children of Midian as prisoners of war. This angers Moses greatly because, as he reminds the Jewish soldiers, the women of Midian helped those of Moab in causing the Jewish men to sin.

Once Moses calms himself, he instructs the soldiers on how to purify themselves from the ritual impurity they contracted from contact with dead bodies during battle. Moses also tells them what they need to do so that they can use things like the non-kosher pots and pans they took from the Midianites after the battle. There are other things the soldiers brought back with them, like cows and donkeys and sheep and even some gold and silver. These are to be divided evenly among the soldiers and everyone else. However, the soldiers are to give a small portion of what they receive (1/500) to Elazar the high priest. Everyone else is to give a portion (1/50) to the Levites.

There is one last task to be done. The army officers count the soldiers who returned from battle. They discover that not a single man was lost in the war. To show gratitude to God for this miracle, the officers donate to the mishkan all the gold jewelry that they personally took from the Midianites.

The story now takes an interesting turn.

The tribes of Reuben and Gad own a lot of cattle. This means that they need a lot of land to graze their flocks. They see that the eastern bank of the Jordan—the lands of Sichon and Og, which they conquered—have lots and lots of land. They therefore ask Moses if they can remain and settle on the eastern bank. Moses is angered by their request. He accuses them of making the same mistake as the spies, who were fearful of the Canaanites and who did not want to enter the land of Canaan.

In an effort to prove to Moses that they are not at all like the spies, the men of Reuben and Gad promise him that they will, of course, join the other tribes when they enter Canaan to conquer the land. They will simply leave their cattle and families behind in fortified cities. Only after all the land has been conquered and settled will they return to the other side of the Jordan.

Moses accepts their offer and informs Joshua and Elazar the High Priest of the agreement. These two tribes, along with half of the tribe of Manasseh, settle on the eastern bank of the Jordan.

Life Lessons from Matot

A major theme that runs through this week's reading is the idea of responsibility. Responsibility is all about our obligations toward our friends and families, toward the community, and even toward ourselves. As you can imagine, this is a topic that has many life lessons attached to it.

The Importance of Keeping Your Word

Pinkie promises. Everyone knows what they are, even adults.[1] A "pinkie promise" is more than a regular promise. It is stronger than

---

1. According to Wikipedia, in the United States, the concept of a "pinky promise" is most common among school-aged children and close friends and

Matot (Num 30:2—32:42)

a regular promise. Making a pinkie promise means that you are really, really, really going to do what you say.

This week's reading talks about pinkie promises, but it doesn't call them that. It instead calls them "vows" and "oaths," and it makes very clear how important it is for a person to keep a vow or an oath.

Our reading makes one other important point about vows and oaths. We may think of them as being very similar or maybe even the same, but, as the Torah makes clear, they are not. Let's explain by using an example of an activity many schools do: a food drive.

There are two ways you can take part in a food drive. You can say, "I'll bring some canned foods to school for the food drive." When you say this, you are obligating yourself to bring cans of food to school. It doesn't matter which cans. You can bring cans of corn or baked beans or cranberry sauce, whatever you think people will like. What matters is that you have committed yourself to doing this. Our reading this week calls this kind of promise a "vow" (*neder* in Hebrew).

There is a second way that you can take part in the food drive. You can say, "I'll bring *this* can of corn to the food drive" or "I'll

---

has existed since at least 1860, when *Dictionary of Americanisms* listed the following accompanying promise:
Pinky, pinky,
Whoever tells a lie
Will sink down to the bad place [sic]
And never rise up again.
But beware! If you shake both pinkies together the promise is fake.

bring *this* can of cranberry sauce to the food drive." Here, your focus is on the object, not on yourself, and our reading calls this an "oath" (*nedavah* in Hebrew).

What does this actually mean? What difference does it really make? Simply this. If you lose the can you said you would donate, or if your parents use it to make dinner, you no longer have an obligation to take part in the food drive. The specific can you set aside is gone, and while it may be nice or even proper to bring a different can, you don't have to. That's how oaths work. But when you make a vow and promise that *you* will bring something, you must bring something, because you (and not the can you lost) are the focus of your promise.

The difference between oaths and vows can be complicated—so complicated that an entire volume of the Talmud is devoted to this topic. But the Jewish view on oaths and vows can be summarized in a single saying of King Solomon.[2] Solomon is said to have written a book called *Ecclesiastes*, in which he shares much of what he learned in life with the Jewish people. Here is what he has to say about promises: "Better that you not vow than that you should vow and not fulfill."[3] In other words, don't make promises you can't keep.

This is the life lesson our reading is teaching us this week. Whether it is an oath or a vow or even a pinkie promise, you should always keep your word and do what you promise.

> *Did you ever keep a promise even though it was really hard? How did that make you feel?*

---

2. Solomon was the son of King David. Once he became king upon his father's death, Solomon carried out the dream of his father by building the temple (960 B.C.E.) The midrash says that Solomon was such a great and righteous person that God offered him anything he wanted. Solomon chose wisdom, which is why Jewish tradition considers him the wisest of men. It is worth noting that God recognized Solomon's wise choice and therefore also granted him great wealth.

3. Ecc 5:4.

Matot (Num 30:2—32:42)

The Importance of Community

In the opening chapter of this book, we discussed the idea of good individuals and good communities. We returned to the idea of community in the story of Korah, where we saw that the tribe of Reuben got caught up in Korah's rebellion because they were his neighbors. (Talk about a lesson in the dangers of being involved in a bad community!) This week's reading gives us a chance to again talk about community, but here we will examine the obligations individuals have to their community as well as the obligations the community has towards its members.

From a Jewish perspective, it is important to be part of a community, as the talmudic sages stated so simply and clearly: "Do not separate yourself from the community."[4] Being part of a community carries with it certain responsibilities, and perhaps none is more central than keeping the community safe. This is just what the soldiers who go to war in this week's reading are doing: keeping their community safe.

In our time, we often refer to soldiers as "first responders," meaning that they are the first to step up when the community faces danger. There are many others who also step up, whom we also call "first responders": people like firefighters and police officers and doctors and nurses. Ask your parents about the bravery they saw among first responders on 9/11. And think about the bravery and sacrifices you read about and perhaps even saw displayed by the first responders who worked so hard to fight the COVID-19 pandemic.

Not all of us are called upon to perform such tasks, but we all have an obligation to protect and improve our communities as best we can. Maybe this means volunteering to clean up a local park so that everyone can enjoy its beauty. Or maybe it's volunteering at a local food bank to help ensure that all members of our community have food to eat. It could even be something as simple as waiting for the light to turn green before you cross the street. By doing so, you keep yourself and people driving on the street safe.

---

4. Pirkei Avot 2:4.

The other key aspect of community we see in this week's reading involves the responsibility of the community toward its members. The soldiers who went to war against the armies of Midian risked their lives protecting the Jewish people. The community thanks them by allowing the soldiers to keep the animals and other valuable items they found after defeating the soldiers of Midian.[5]

What a nice thing to do. What an unsurprising thing to do. Rewarding those who risk their lives for others. But what comes next? God wants to remind the soldiers that even when they are rewarded by the community, they still have an obligation to support the community. He therefore commands the soldiers to share what they captured in the war (a 50/50 split) with those members of the community who did not go to war.

It is, in a sense, a never-ending circle. The people support the community, which supports the people, who, in turn, again support the community. The talmudic rabbis understood how critical this circle is to the very idea of community. They describe it this way: "All who labor with [or for] the community should labor with [or for] them for the sake Heaven."[6] In other words, we should serve the community not for the sake of honor or money but for the sake of Heaven.[7] Why? Because it's the correct thing to do. It's also what God wants and expects us to do.

> *What is one thing you and your family do to support the community? Why did you choose this thing?*

5. Another example of the community's obligations toward those who defend it is found in chapter 20 (verses 5–7) of Deuteronomy. There, prior to going to war, a priest is to address the soldiers. He is to say to them: "Is there anyone who has built a new house but has not dedicated it? Let him go back to his home, lest he die in battle and another dedicate it. Is there anyone who has planted a vineyard but has never harvested it? Let him go back to his home, lest he die in battle and another harvest it. Is there anyone who has paid the bride-price for a wife, but who has not yet married her? Let him go back to his home, lest he die in battle and another marry her." In other words, those men who have begun the next chapter in their lives are permitted to enjoy and benefit from them prior to risking it all in war.

6. Pirkei Avot 2:2.

7. For a fuller explanation of this phrase, go back to our discussion in the chapter on Korah.

Matot (Num 30:2—32:42)

In what ways does your community support you and your family?

The Importance of Sticking Together

We now come to a story that builds upon what we learned about the importance of keeping your word and upon the importance of community. It is a story that has much to teach us about the importance of the Jewish people sticking together. Or, as adults might describe it, the importance of unity.

Let's review the main points of the story. The Jewish people have reached the border of Canaan, the land promised to their forefathers Abraham, Isaac, and Jacob. Plans are being made for crossing the Jordan River and conquering the land. While these plans are being discussed, members of the tribes of Reuben and Gad approach Moses with a request that greatly displeases him. It seems that these two tribes have very large flocks, with large numbers of cattle and sheep. From their perspective, the east side of the Jordan River, where they are right now, looks perfect. It has many large pastures where their animals can graze, and they want Moses's permission to settle on this side of the Jordan and not cross into Canaan with the other tribes.

Moses can't believe what he is hearing. He angrily responds: "Are your brothers to go to war while you stay here?" The two tribes try again to explain their reasons for making this request. After what seems to be a long argument, Moses agrees. Here's why.

First, the tribes of Reuben and Gad give Moses their word. They promise that they will cross over the Jordan and take part in the conquest of Canaan. To show Moses how serious they are, the men of these tribes leave their families and their flocks behind while they take part in the war. And by the way, according to the midrash, the men were away for fourteen years: seven years to fight the war and another seven years to divide up the land properly.

Second, after speaking with Moses, they recognize that they have a responsibility to the community. They understand and accept that the other tribes need them to join in the war.

Third, and most important, they finally see how important it is for all the tribes to stick together, even if some of them are living on the one side of the Jordan River while most of them cross that river. Moses reminds them about what happened the last time the Jewish people were so close to the border of Canaan, almost forty years ago. At that time, the people asked Moses to send spies to scout out the land. Moses agreed, but when the people heard the report of the spies, their unity crumbled. Some believed that they should move forward into Canaan. Most were afraid of doing so and refused. Moses's point to the tribes of Reuben and Gad is this: We missed a chance once before to conquer and settle in the land of Canaan because we weren't unified. Now, if you don't stick with us and join the war, we will again risk missing our chance.

As we know, they did not miss their chance. This reminds us that when people keep their word, when they accept their responsibilities toward one another, and when they stick together, good things usually follow.

> *Can you think of a time when your family or your classmates all joined together to do something? What made you stick together? Did you accomplish your goal? Why or why not?*

Matot (Num 30:2—32:42)

Now, try to think of a time when your family or your classmates tried to join together to do something but couldn't stick together. Why was that?

Massei

(Num 33:1—36:13)

Summary of This Week's Reading

The Hebrew name of this week's reading, Massei, *means "travels" or "journeys." It's a very appropriate name because our reading lists the forty-two journeys the Jewish people made during their forty years in the Sinai wilderness. These journeys took them all the way from Egypt to the Jordan River, which marked the border of the land of Canaan.*

God now instructs the Jewish people that after crossing the river, they are to conquer all the people living in Canaan and destroy their idols. God also tells them what the borders of their new homeland of Israel will be.

Per God's command, the land itself is to be divided by lottery among the tribes, with nine and a half tribes crossing the Jordan River to settle on its western bank (in what today is the land of Israel). The rest (Reuben, Gad, and half of the tribe of Manasseh) will remain and settle on the eastern bank of the Jordan. (This area in our times is the country of Jordan.)

Once the lottery is complete, each tribe's portion is to be divided among all the members of the tribe. The people who do this are appointed by God Himself.

What about the tribe of Levi? Their inheritance, as we have seen, is to work in the mishkan. This means they receive no portion of the land. Where will they live? God of course did not forget the tribe of Levi, and He commands the other tribes to give the Levites forty-eight cities where they can live. Along with these cities, the Levites are given large areas of land surrounding the cities for their cattle.

Our reading this week closes with a discussion of the daughters of the Zelophehad, who asked for and received their own portions in the land of Canaan. The leaders of Zelophehad's tribe themselves have a question. If these five women married men from a different tribe, their sons, who would be members of their fathers' tribes, would inherit their mothers' properties from the tribe of Zelophehad upon their deaths. This would mean that these properties would become part of their portions of their fathers' tribes, and this would mean that the territory of Zelophehad's tribe would become smaller. To avoid this problem, God instructs Zelophehad's daughters to marry men from their own tribe so that the land they inherit and ultimately pass on to their children will remain with their tribe.

Life Lessons from Massei

Given that this is the last reading in Numbers, it's not surprising that it reviews and recaps the journeys of the Jewish people through the Sinai wilderness. The same is true for the life lessons we find in this reading. In a way, they will review and recap much of what we've learned in this book.

A Sign for the Children

There is an interesting concept in Judaism that is very much present in this week's reading. The Hebrew for this concept is *ma'aseh avot siman levanim*. This phrase is generally translated as "the actions of the forefathers are a symbol (or sign) for the children." Let's give a few examples to explain what this really means.

We know from the book of Genesis that Abraham, Isaac, and Jacob each offered sacrifices to God as a way of worshipping God, even though they were not commanded to do so. In the future, first in the mishkan and then in the temple in Jerusalem, their descendants used this form of worship they had learned from their ancestors. We see here that the sacrifices of the patriarchs were

Massei (Num 33:1—36:13)

signs for their descendants. More than that, they were examples of what the descendants would themselves do in the future.

Consider also the story from Genesis about Abraham and Sarah going down to Egypt when a great famine strikes the land of Israel. Upon their arrival in Egypt, the king's soldiers are awed by Sarah's beauty. They kidnap Sarah and bring her to the king. But, as the midrash tells us, before Pharoah (the kings of Egypt are always called "Pharoah" in the Torah) can harm or even touch Sarah, he is struck by plagues, just as his descendants would be as punishment for enslaving the Jewish people. (Yes, we are referring to the ten plagues that struck Egypt when Pharoah refused to let the Jewish people leave.) Yet another sign for future generations.

What these examples show us (and there are many more such examples in the Torah) is that the stories about the patriarchs and the matriarchs are in the Bible so we can learn from our ancestors' actions. *Ma'aseh avot siman levanim* means that the actions of the forefathers are, in a very real sense, a symbol for the children, which brings us to this week's reading.

There is another well-known midrash about Abraham and Sarah's visit to Egypt, one that describes the many stops they made in the Sinai wilderness on their way back to the land of Israel. According to this midrash, the places where Abraham and Sarah stopped are the same places where Moses and the Jewish people encamped during their forty years in the Sinai wilderness. Here we have yet another very real sign for the children.

If the actions of our forefathers are truly to be signs for us, we must carefully study stories such as the ones we have just mentioned. They are there for us to read, discuss, and eventually relate to our everyday lives. And if we are successful in our efforts and make these lessons part of our own daily lives, we will in turn be able to make them signs and symbols for our descendants.

> *Ask your parents about a "sign" that was passed down to them by their parents. What makes this sign so special to them? Have they passed it on to you yet?*

A Few Final Thoughts

As we reach the end of Numbers, we have seen that it has many complex stories that are difficult to explain. However, this is not just the case for Numbers. It is true for all the books of the Torah. Take Genesis as an example.

There is so much for us to learn from the creation story, but do any of us really understand how creation actually happened? Can any of us comprehend what the verse is telling us when it says, "God said, 'Let there be light'; and there was light"?

Then there is the story of Noah and the flood. Again, so much to learn, but how did the animals know to make their way to Noah and his ark? And how did certain animals know to come in pairs while others came in groups of seven?[1]

If you took a few minutes, you could probably come up with a long list of interesting and important questions about many of the stories in Genesis. (In fact, why don't you try to come up with two right now?)

Next comes the book of Exodus. Exodus leaves us with even more questions. How did the plagues work? How did God split the Sea of Reeds? And we can't even begin to list all the unanswerable questions about God's revelation at Mount Sinai.

The book of Numbers is different. It, too, has many difficult stories that leave us searching for answers. But the questions we struggle with regarding Numbers tend not to be, "How did this happen?" More often, we ask *why*, as in, "Why did the people do that?" Or "What could they possibly have been thinking when they did that?"

These are the types of questions we need to ask when we read about the spies or Korah's rebellion or Balaam's attempts to curse the Jewish people. We certainly ask such questions when we read about the people's complaints about the manna and when we read about the golden calf.

---

1. While most of the animals came in pairs of male and female, some arrived in in groups of seven. Noah uses animals from these groups of seven of offer sacrifices to God once the flood is over and he and his family are safe.

Massei (Num 33:1—36:13)

Learning to ask such questions and learning to accept that there may not be good answers is what this book has been all about.

If you are a curious student but are sometimes a little shy or nervous about asking questions, I hope this book showed you the value of asking, especially when you are confronted with stories you don't quite understand.

If, on the other hand, you are the type of person who likes asking questions and who is not afraid to ask hard questions, I like to believe this book showed you how right you are to ask your questions.

When I think about asking questions (and, for the record, I am always among the first to raise my hand to ask a question), I believe Rabbi Jonathan Sacks, who for many years served as the Chief Rabbi of England, said it best: "In Judaism, to be without questions is not a sign of faith, but of lack of depth."[2]

Rabbi Sacks had even more to say when it came to children asking questions. He notes that there is an old English proverb that states, "Children should be seen, not heard." He also reminds us about the famous Christian saying "Children, be obedient to your parents in all things, for this is well-pleasing to the LORD."[3] But, says Rabbi Sacks, "In Judaism the opposite is the case. It is a religious duty to teach our children to ask questions. That is how they grow."[4]

May you always be asking and growing. And by doing so, may you become a role model for your friends today and for your own children at some point in the future.

---

2. Sacks, "The Art of Asking Questions."
3. Colossians 3:20.
4. Sacks, "The Necessity of Asking Questions."

About the Author

Rabbi Reuven Travis earned his bachelor's degree from Dartmouth College, where he graduated Phi Beta Kappa, with a double major in French literature and political science. He holds a master's degree in teaching from Mercer University and also earned a master's in Judaic studies from Spertus College. He received his rabbinic ordination from Rabbi Michael J. Broyde, dean of the Atlanta Torah MITzion Kollel, after spending four years studying with Rabbi Broyde and the members of the kollel.

Rabbi Travis worked in Jewish day schools for 20 years and taught students from second grade through high school. He has previously published three scholarly works on the book of Job, the book of Numbers, and the book of Genesis, respectively, and is currently working on a number of new book projects. He also teaches online classes on topics ranging from the Bible to Jewish medical ethics to American history.

Bibliography

McAlpine, Fraser. "Lost in Translation: Five British Stereotypes That Are True." Anglophenia (blog). http://www.bbcamerica.com/anglophenia/2011/09/lost-in-translation-five-british-stereotypes-that-are-true

Olson, Carl. ""The 'Angry God' and the 'Loving God.'" *Our Sunday Visitor*. April 4, 2013. https://www.osv.com/Article/TabId/493/ArtMID/13569/ArticleID/9385/The-"Angry-God"-and-the-"Loving-God"-.aspx

Ramban (Nahmanides). *The Disputation at Barcelona*. Translated by Charles B. Chavel. New York: Shilo, 1983.

Sacks, Jonathan. "The Art of Asking Questions." Rohr Jewish Learning Institute. https://lessons.myjli.com/why/index.php/2016/11/30/the-art-of-asking-questions/.

———. "The Necessity of Asking Questions." OU Torah. https://outorah.org/p/861/.

Schäferhoff, Nick. "9 German Stereotypes That Are Straight Up True." FluentU (blog). https://www.fluentu.com/blog/german/german-stereotypes/

Sforno, Ovadiah ben Yaacov. *Commentary on the Torah*. Translated by Raphael Pelcovitz. Brooklyn, NY: Mesorah, 1987.

Swindoll, Charles. "Numbers." The Bible-Teaching Ministry of Charles R. Swindoll. https://www.insight.org/resources/bible/the-pentateuch/numbers

Terracciano, Antonio, and Robert R. McCrae. "Perceptions of Americans and the Iraq Invasion: Implications for Understanding National Character Stereotypes." *Journal of Cross Cultural Psychology* 38, no. 6 (2007): 695–710. Author manuscript available online at https://www.ncbi.nlm.nih.gov/pmc/articles/PMC2447921/#!po=24.0909

www.ingramcontent.com/pod-product-compliance
Lightning Source LLC
Chambersburg PA
CBHW072152160426
43197CB00012B/2350